HOLLI MOE

FINDING THE
MISSING
MILLIONS
IN M&A

How to Maximize Value and Minimize
Regret in Every Transaction

SILVERSMITH
PRESS

Published by Silversmith Press–Houston, Texas
www.silversmithpress.com

ISBN 978-1-967386-38-3 (Softcover Book)
ISBN 978-1-967386-50-5 (Hardcover Book)
ISBN 978-1-967386-39-0 (eBook)

Dedication

To **Adam E. Coffey:** My mentor and teacher.
You believed in me, gave me a chance,
and helped me find my path. I am forever grateful.
To **Joanna Hunt and Silversmith Press**:
Rare talent, rare spirit.
You took my little M&A field guide and gave it wings.
Your gift preserves my legacy and lifts my voice.
To **my family**—my inspiration, my heart.
I love you all.

FOREWORD

BY ADAM E. COFFEY

4x Bestselling Author, Veteran CEO, and
Acclaimed Expert in Private Equity & Business Growth

I first met Holli at my country club for lunch. She was a new member of my Chairman's Group and at the time, she was in between roles—an ex-CFO who had been doing M&A like me. I could tell right away that she was highly skilled. She was also at a crossroads wondering: *do I go back to the corporate world, or do I do something different?* It didn't take long for me to see the answer. I told her to hang up her shingle right away because there's a gaping hole in the market for her skillset.

You see, when I start looking at a company to buy, the first thing I want to do is review the financial statements and apply my 30/20/10 rule. And here's what I already know going in: CEOs don't know their numbers. Why? Because QuickBooks doesn't know their numbers. In all my years, I've never reviewed a single company with truly clean, proper financials. Not one. That's because the entire bookkeeping world is designed for one purpose: to calculate revenue so you can pay taxes. And taxes have nothing to do with valuation.

So the first thing I need is to get a clear financial picture. That's where Holli comes in. Holli is the kind of financial leader every CEO and every investor wants by their side. She can make sense of deal chaos. She can turn a jumbled mess of numbers into a story that's clear, actionable, and true. Holli makes the "gauges on the ship" work so CEOs can actually steer with clarity and confidence.

Most CEOs are like me: strong on vision and operations, but not financial experts. We rely heavily on strong CFOs who can make the numbers speak, who can take financial planning and analysis and turn it into insight. That's Holli's superpower. I've never met anyone who understands financials the way Holli does. As a CFO, she doesn't "do the books" she uncovers the story inside them. She sees what others miss—whether it's hidden risk, untapped opportunity, or millions of dollars quietly slipping away.

Not only is Holli a gifted CFO and CPA, she's also a gifted teacher. I've had Holli speak at my conferences and thankfully, she doesn't drown you in accounting jargon. She makes learning fun and memorable, and that's what you will experience in this book. Holli will show you how to read the story behind the numbers. She will give you the tools to cut through the noise, minimize regret, and approach deals with clarity and discipline. And she will do it with humor, candor, and a style that will keep you turning pages.

There's a lot of "fluff" books out there disguised as business books. This isn't one of them. Holli has lived in this world. She's guided companies through exits, she's found the missing millions, and now she's giving you the playbook. If you're serious about understanding how to create value and protect it—whether you're an entrepreneur, a CEO, or an investor—you're holding the right book in your hands.

Dig in. Learn from Holli. And when you finish, I promise you'll never look at a financial statement the same way again. More importantly, you'll never approach a deal the same way again, either.

CONTENTS

Section 3

Section 4

INTRODUCTION

WELCOME TO THE WILD WORLD OF M&A!

What if the most expensive mistake in Mergers & Acquisitions (M&A) isn't failure—but success followed by regret? Can you imagine walking away from an M&A transaction only to *later learn* you left millions on the table—even after months, or years of negotiations, preparation, and due diligence?

It happens all the time. I've seen it personally.

Why? Because many buyers and sellers *believe* they're prepared. They've read the books, listened to the podcasts, and maybe even hired a broker. But that's not the same as being "deal-ready" and knowing what to look out for. A broker can market your business, but the broker is not the one finding the hidden millions buried in the numbers. And even if you've been through a deal or two, most company owners won't come close to doing enough transactions in a lifetime to reach true expert level. Not because they aren't smart or capable—far from it. It's because M&A is a world you must live in every day to see all the angles, patterns, and strategies buyers and investors use to capture value.

With over three decades in the financial services arena, let me tell you: M&A is not for the faint of heart. It's complicated, emotional, and brutally punishing to anyone who walks in unprepared, or worse—mis-prepared. We have all been there at some point in life, *thinking* we were ready for something only to find out the hard way, we were not. (Public speaking anyone?) I call this "confident ignorance" and it abounds in M&A. This is when you confidently know what you know, but you don't have a clue there's still a lot more to know beyond that. And in this world, if you get it wrong, the fallout isn't theoretical— it's financial, reputational, and deeply personal. Worst of all, one mistake, one oversight, one missed number can literally cost millions of dollars.

So, how do you mitigate risk and regret? Stay tuned.

M&A is way more than crunching numbers in a black and white sales transaction. It's a high-stakes negotiation where the rules shift with every conversation. And the stakes are far higher than most people realize when they begin. Why? Because business isn't just numbers and contracts—it's a living, breathing story. Years of sweat equity, late nights, and gut-wrenching decisions are woven into every line of the P&L. If you've built a company, you know the real value of it is *intangibly more* than what can be measured on a spreadsheet. You've led teams, taken risks, fought with heart, skipped paychecks, fired your family, and shouldered pressure few understand. The hard truth about entrepreneurship is this:

In year one, about 22% of new businesses fail.

By year five, 50% are gone.

By year ten, 65% have closed.

And by year fifteen, 73% have disappeared.

If your business has survived this far, congratulations! But don't get comfortable yet. Exiting isn't a smooth ride into the sunset. Even if you are ready to hand over the reins, that stats show 70% of businesses that go to market *never find a buyer.* And of the deals that do close, many fall short of expectations for both sellers and buyers primarily because they don't know what they don't know.

Now let me give you the good news: this doesn't have to be you. Whether this is your very first look at M&A, your tenth deal, or you're already advising others, this book was written to meet you where you are and take you further. There's a reason this book found its way into your hands. Whether you're a seller looking to exit with confidence, a buyer hoping to grow strategically, or an expert in the field looking to expand your skillset, you are in the right place. I wrote this book because after decades of advising CEOs, buyers, and sellers, I've seen the same mistakes play out again and again. I've been a part of deals worth hundreds of millions of dollars and I've seen how the smallest oversight can erase value or even derail the whole transaction. And it happens even when key players are experienced in M&A. I know this because not only do I advise my clients through all stages of the process, but I'm also called in as a financial expert for transactions guided by other industry experts. When the stakes are highest, when the numbers don't add up, when risks hide in plain sight—when both sides can't put the pieces of the puzzle together, that's where I come in. I help uncover risks, fix broken financial stories, look around corners, avoid regret, and find the missing millions.

Over the years, I've developed a system and framework for the way I approach M&A that's different from anyone else I've encountered in this arena. I look at things differently, so I see things others miss. This is what sets me apart in the industry and this is what I'm going to teach you. On top of that, my C-level background isn't just in financial services, it's in IT and operations, which broadens my lens for finding real-world value in companies. This book isn't theory. It's a trail map built from real experience with real deals—deals that nearly collapsed, deals that exceeded expectations, and deals that changed lives. I wrote it so you could enter this process eyes wide open—with clarity, control, and zero regrets.

Maybe this isn't your first rodeo. Maybe you've won big already, or you've made mistakes you don't want to repeat. No matter where you are in the M&A process, no matter the size of your business, your background, or expertise, this book is for you. You've come this far, and you deserve the power to shape your story on your terms and maximize the value in your M&A transactions.

Now, let me warn you, this will not be like any other M&A book you've ever read. If you've attended one of my trainings or seminars, you know that I much prefer fun things like parades over boring spreadsheets—and this book might feel like a little of both. If we've never met—hello and welcome! The pleasure is all mine.

THE M&A STORY

Before we get too far, we must explore the power of a story. Yes, a story. Stories are inherently powerful. Every decision we make, every belief we have, every action we take starts with a story. Maybe growing up you had a parent read you a story before bed. Maybe a loved one told you a story that wasn't true. In each scenario, the story had the power to impact your thoughts, feelings, and actions. And that's what stories do. Stories shape our lives. We hear stories every day, and we tell stories every day. While all stories are powerful, the *most* powerful story is the one you tell yourself because the story you tell yourself is the one you will live. *But wait a minute Holli...* *what does any of this have to do with M&A? Can't we just get to* *the missing millions?*

I'm so glad you asked. Let me explain.

You see, stories are a very important part of the M&A process because every person involved shows up with a story, and the M&A deal you are crafting is in fact a merger of these stories. Most people look at M&A as a one-dimensional sales transaction, made up of numbers, spreadsheets, and assets, but nothing could be further from the truth. In my world, a deal is made up of stories. When others look at spreadsheets and financial statements, they see numbers—dollars and cents, which makes sense. However, when I look at spreadsheets and financial statements I see *stories*. Yes, numbers tell a story—and it's not just a story about the relationship of the numbers, it's a story about the business, the management, and about the philosophy of the owners. The story in the numbers informs the buyer on whether or not they should proceed and how. You may have heard it said that success leaves clues—well in M&A the numbers leave clues. That's why I called this book, *Finding the Missing Millions.* Because if you look carefully enough at the clues and you understand how to put the M&A story together, you can see what's missing—which may quite literally equate to millions of dollars to your bottom line.

Now something very interesting just happened to you and you probably aren't even aware of it. You see, by exploring this concept of stories in M&A—two things that seem so completely unrelated out of context—I just created a pattern interrupt in your brain. By creating a pattern interrupt which means you are now teed up for more efficient learning, and to see the whole M&A process differently—which is the goal of this book. Excellent! Your brain is ready, and you are now in a state of learning.

So, lesson number one: Numbers tell stories.

Lesson number two: Holli also tells stories.

That's because Holli is a CPA who likes to have fun, because fun equals the best way to learn. And to help you train your brain to look for stories, I'm going to be using stories a lot in this book. Yes, I use real life M&A examples, but I also use what I call my "Mock-Tale" or made-up stories, analogies, and metaphors designed for the sole purpose of helping you understand and remember what I'm teaching. I guess you could say, it's always happy hour somewhere . . . but especially when I'm teaching! Cheers!

Now, the difference between a good deal and a great one isn't luck—it's insight, intention, and the discipline to see what others miss. So, sharpen your pencil and open your mind! It's time to get to work and go find your missing millions.

(Don't you just love the sound of that?)

CHAPTER 1

THE DEAL FRONTIER

MAPPING SUCCESS IN THE HIGH-STAKES WORLD OF M&A

Today's surge in mergers and acquisitions (M&A) isn't just coincidence, it's economics. Across industries, thousands of fragmented, owner–operated businesses are changing hands as Baby Boomer founders prepare to retire. Buyers, especially first-time acquirers and small private equity groups, see a rare and exciting opportunity—the chance to buy a business at a lower multiple, grow it organically or through additional acquisitions, and eventually sell it for a much higher multiple. Simply put, bigger companies are worth more—not just because of their size, but because of the perceived reduction in risk which is why acquiring smaller companies and merging them is so attractive. This is the power of *arbitrage*: when you buy at a value of three times earnings, and then sell at eight, you capture the spread through scale, systems, and sophistication which translates to millions, and potentially billions.

Understanding this dynamic is essential for both buyers and sellers who want to position their businesses for maximum value in today's market. And if you want to play the M&A game you have to understand the rules. The problem is that many sellers and buyers set out to build their empires and they don't even fully understand the game. Don't worry, you're in the right place. The landscape of M&A is not one to be traveled lightly, or unprepared and so understanding the "Deal Frontier" is where we begin . . .

A TALE OF TWO RIDERS (A MOCK-TALE, THAT IS)

The sun had just crested the horizon when two riders met at the edge of town. One carried years of grit in his saddlebag—contracts, customers, and memories of sleepless nights that carved deep lines into his face. He wasn't just holding numbers; he was holding a lifetime of bets, wins, and scars.

> IF YOU WANT TO PLAY THE M&A GAME, YOU HAVE TO UNDERSTAND THE RULES.

The other arrived fresh, spreadsheets tucked under his arm like a lasso, eyes sharp with ambition. He'd devoured podcasts on buying businesses, chewed up M&A headlines and believed whole-heartedly he was ready for the ride.

Both riders thought they knew the terrain. Both believed they were prepared. But just beyond the dusty horizon lay a canyon of uncharted territory—questions unasked and answers unknown, waiting to swallow them both.

In M&A, the greatest mistake is thinking you can start with the numbers. You cannot. Numbers may tell a story, but the story begins long before the math.

SETTING YOUR COMPASS

A deal can go off-course right from the start—not because the numbers are wrong, but because the compass is. Numbers are not your compass. Perspective is. Most sellers think the compass is price. Most buyers think it's the books. Both are wrong. Before you chase EBITDA(Earnings before Interest Taxes Depreciation and Amortization) or balance sheets, you need to see the whole map. The terrain is emotional, strategic, and financial. Ignore one, and the others will mislead you and derail your deal. Set your compass first. Once you orient to the bigger picture, the path through every deal comes into focus.

THE M&A TRAIL MAP: FROM FIRST STEP TO FINAL SUNSET

Every deal is a journey. Some paths are well-worn, others are unmarked. The smart buyer or seller doesn't just ride out blindly—they carry a map. Not a literal one, but a framework that shows the terrain ahead: the cliffs to avoid, the turns to watch, and the water holes that can keep you alive. This book is that map. Every chapter is a stop along the trail. Keep it close so you can return to it when the deal dust rises.

Not only do you need your map, but you also need to learn the language. But don't worry—I'll help you speak it fluently. I will explain industry terms as we go along but anytime you need a quick refresher, flip to *Holli's M&A Survival Glossary* at the back of this book.

Now, back to the map—this book is broken down into stages that mirror the stages of a deal. Breaking down the process will help you clearly see what you need at each step.

Stage 1: Preparation: Packing Your Saddlebag (Ch. 1–5)
Before you ever sign an LOI, you need to get your "gear" in order.

- **Knowing the Deal Frontier** → Setting your compass and seeing the whole landscape.

- **Negotiating the Unseen** → What's not on the spreadsheets kill more deals than anything else.
- **The Numbers Tell Stories** → How financials whisper truths about behavior, not just math.
- **EBITDA Basics** → How to prep, normalize, and calculate without fooling yourself.
- **What Can I Afford?** → Buyers face the reality check: EBITDA doesn't pay debt, cash flow does.

Stage 2: Choosing Your Route—LOI & Early Terms (Ch. 6–9)
Once you're ready to ride, you choose your direction. This is where intentions turn into offers.

- **The Value Chessboard & PE Math**→ Finding millions overnight!
- **Deal Structures** → Asset vs. stock, tax myths, and why structure changes everything.
- **Creative Carve-Outs** → Not every path means buying the whole company—sometimes you only take the slice that matters.

Stage 3: Navigating the Dealbreakers (Ch. 10–11)
The terrain gets rough and this is where most travelers get snakebit.

- **Working Capital** → The dance no one wants to learn, but everyone must.
- **Diligence** → The trenches where red flags, fatigue, and deal-killing details surface.

Stage 4: Closing Mechanics (Ch. 12–13)
By now you've crossed rivers, survived storms, and the finish line is near. But before you celebrate, you need protection.

- **Earnouts** → Marriage, divorce, and everything in between. The clause of hope and heartbreak.
- **Cover Your Tail** → Why tail insurance matters more than trust.

Stage 5: New Homestead—Post-Close (Ch. 14–15)
The papers are signed. The real work begins.

- **Taking Care of Employees** → People are the oxygen of a deal. Get this wrong, and the campfire goes cold.
- **Integration** → The beautiful chaos you can plan for—the hundred-day collision and beyond.

Stage 6: Sunset Reflections—Lessons & Red Flags (Ch. 16–17)
When the dust settles, what remains are the lessons and the scars.

- **Red Flags** → How to see the warning signs before they trip you, and how to walk away with clarity.
- **Discipline that Builds Empires** → Finding the missing millions. Numbers close deals, but emotions, discipline, and trust are what keep them whole.

THE NUMBERS STILL MATTER

By now you might be thinking: *"Holli, this sounds like a cowboy tale—where are my spreadsheets?"* Hold your horses.

The numbers are coming. They're the backbone of every deal. But numbers only make sense when you understand the terrain they sit on. Without context, spreadsheets are just scenery with no map.

THE BOTTOM LINE

This is your trail map. Revisit it often. Grab your ledger. Steady your reins. The trail ahead is wild, but with this map, you won't lose your way—or your millions—in the canyons of confusion.

CHAPTER 2

NEGOTIATING THE UNSEEN

THE BIGGEST VARIABLE IN M&A
ISN'T FINANCIAL.

It hit me in an airport. Gate C12, middle of the night. Cold coffee in one hand, a redlined LOI in the other. Two strong businesses, a clean model, EBITDA margins that sang—but no deal. The seller had gone silent. The buyer was unraveling. And I was stuck in the middle, staring at numbers that should have worked, realizing—*this isn't about EBITDA anymore.*

The spreadsheet was perfect.

The humans were not.

It wasn't margins, multiples, or deal math. It was fear, ego. grief, and pride—things no spreadsheet could model. That was the moment I learned the biggest variable in M&A isn't financial. It's human.

That's when everything changed. That's when I learned the story isn't about spreadsheets. That's when I stopped being the clean-financials-closer and started becoming the operator who listens for what *isn't* being said. It didn't take a degree in psychology, it took paying attention.

ATG SYNDROME

Ever study Alexander the Great in school? Brilliant strategist. Conquered the known world by age thirty. But his empire fractured within years of his death—not because of bad math, but because of unchecked emotions: ego, paranoia, and pride.

I call this ATG Syndrome. And I see it in deals all the time. Fear shows up as retrades. Ego turns diligence into combat. Shame hides in sloppy ledgers. Grief makes sellers cling to receivables like life preservers. The danger isn't the emotion itself—it's ignoring it. That's when value evaporates. No one talks about this part. But it's why so many deals quietly die—or survive-you have to learn to negotiate the unseen first. Let's take a look at five emotional patterns that rise up in the deal process and how to navigate them.

> THE DANGER ISN'T THE EMOTION ITSELF—IT'S IGNORING IT. THAT'S WHEN VALUE EVAPORATES. YOU HAVE TO LEARN TO NEGOTIATE THE UNSEEN FIRST.

1. COLD FEET AT CLOSE

I was in month twelve of negotiations on this deal, and sick in every sense of the word. Literally. Deals are exhausting at the best of times, but this one had dragged on for so long that even my body gave out—I had pneumonia. Just when I thought we were at the finish line, the seller started dragging old terms back on the table. Terms we had closed months earlier were suddenly "open for discussion." Here we all were, back at the closing table again. His wife was pushing him to hold firm. I was furious. Feverish, coughing, worn down, I wanted to slam my hand on the table and shout, *"We already settled this!"*

At the time, I thought it was greed. A power play. But looking back, that wasn't it at all. It was fear. He was staring down the finality of letting go of his life's work. His wife mirrored and amplified his emotion. It wasn't that they were trying to squeeze the last nickel out of the deal—they were trying to make peace with the goodbye. It showed up like indecision and delay. I finally closed the deal but it was more of a bumpy ride than it needed to be. If I had this understanding at the time, I could have shown up differently. In the moment, I met fear with impatience, but what the circumstance needed was compassion. Had I affirmed the seller's position and acknowledge the difficulty of letting go, we might have had a smoother ride to the closing table.

2. DILIGENCE PANIC

I once worked with a seller who, every time I asked a financial question, unraveled into a long, shaky explanation. Nothing lined up neatly. I saw red flags everywhere and it looked like he was hiding something. Turns out he was. When the QofE arrived, he walked in with his "books," which turned out to be a hand typed ledger. On a typewriter, no less. My first reaction was disbelief. But as I listened to him explain things, I realized: he knew his numbers. Every line, every penny. He was just ashamed— ashamed of his outdated systems, afraid of being judged under a microscope. He knew his systems were antiquated but he just didn't know how to do it any other way.

What I had mistaken for dishonesty or fraud was really embarrassment. Shame hides behind defensiveness the same way dishonesty does. The difference is that shame can be met with patience and dignity preserved which leads to better outcomes for all parties involved. That seller didn't need me to push harder. He needed me to slow down.

3. THE WORKING CAPITAL FIGHT

I once supported a buyer acquiring a distribution company. On paper, everything looked fine. But the seller—and his wife—dug their heals in: "We are not leaving working capital. Period." No logic. No compromise.

We modeled scenarios. We explained the mechanics. Nothing worked. They had bought their business years earlier from someone who stripped it bare—no receivables, no inventory. They lived through the trauma of starting with nothing, and they refused to listen to any logic. At the end of the day, the argument wasn't really about accounts receivable. It was about old, festering wounds.

In hindsight, I should have started with education earlier. Maybe even stories instead of spreadsheets. Because once fear hardens into defiance, you're not talking about balance sheets anymore. You're talking about unseen monsters and scars and those are very difficult to negotiate with!

4. SPREADSHEET TUNNEL VISION

Early in my career, I believed results lived inside the cells of an Excel sheet. If I could model faster, reconcile tighter, and deliver the cleanest work, I was winning. I skipped lunch. I dodged hallway conversations. Every unbilled minute felt like wasted time. But deals aren't closed by spreadsheets alone. They're closed by people. And people remember how you made them feel long after they forget your EBITDA calc.

The irony is that the best deals I've ever been a part of—the ones that actually stuck—were the ones where I slowed down long enough to have a coffee, to laugh, to listen. Trust builds returns. Numbers only confirm them.

Buyers and sellers: get to know one another before you say, "I do." This may very well be the most important aspect of your deal!

5. THE IDENTITY CRASH AFTER CLOSING

The closing dinner is over. The champagne glasses are empty. The wires have cleared. And then the hangover sets in—not from the alcohol, but from the reality.

The buyer sits at their new desk, staring at the inbox, whispering to themselves: *"Did I overpay? Can I really run this business?"*

The seller sits at their kitchen table, staring at the same inbox, unable to send the farewell email. Both had an entire identity shift in less than twenty-four hours.

You can't model this. No spreadsheet can forecast grief. Deals don't just transfer assets; they uproot people. And even when everyone wins, it still hurts to let go.

I've learned that buyers need room to breathe, and sellers need room to mourn. Even success carries loss. Ignoring that truth only makes the silence heavier.

WHAT I WISH I HAD KNOWN

What I did not realize early in my career is that these were not just "my" challenges—they were patterns. Diligence panic, retrades, working capital tantrums, identity crises—they repeat in deal after deal, no matter who is at the table. Buyers face them. Sellers face them. The details may change, but the emotions and behaviors are universal. Recognizing the pattern early means not being trapped by it.

I used to believe the finish line was the deal itself—that

speed, precision, and the cleanest spreadsheet were the real wins. But what I wish I had known sooner is this: people remember how you made them feel long after they forget your model.

I've led with impatience when compassion was called for. I've confused shame with fraud. I've tried to bulldoze through fear instead of pausing to let people breathe. I've made those mistakes—and they were expensive, not just in dollars but in trust. What I know now is that connection is not fluff. It's a closing strategy. Fear isn't rational, but it is real—and it is sitting across the table from you in every deal. Anger drains value. Empathy creates it.

I'm not pretending I've mastered this. But if you take nothing else from this chapter, take this: you are not just buying or selling a business. You are stepping into someone else's story. And if you don't honor that story, no amount of math will save your deal.

Very often, buyers and sellers are moving so fast through the process, they aren't even aware of what's going on internally, or the story buried deep inside and how it's impacting their decision process. When emotions are high, judgement is low in any scenario of life. Diffusing intense emotions with compassion, patience and understanding may take longer, but it's the glue that holds a deal together.

BOTTOM LINE

I used to believe the hardest part of a deal was the technical part—the numbers, the reps and warranties, the models, etc. But the truth is, the hardest part is invisible. It's what's going on that you can't see—fear, grief, shame, and pride. You can't see these on a term sheet, but they can stall a deal faster than any EBITDA adjustment. Ignore them, and you'll lose more than money. You'll lose trust. And once trust goes missing, the millions follow.

M&A looks like spreadsheets but it feels like identity shifts, power moves, grief, relief, fear, and hope. If you understand this—and really *pay attention* to it—you'll become the kind of leader that people want to sell to, buy from, and work alongside. And that is the greatest edge in deal-making. See the unseen, honor the emotions, and not only will you protect the millions, you'll make them!

> YOU ARE NOT JUST BUYING OR SELLING A BUSINESS. YOU ARE STEPPING INTO SOMEONE ELSE'S STORY.

CHAPTER 3

THE ART OF READING A BUSINESS

NOT ONLY DO NUMBERS TELL STORIES, BUT THEY ARE ALSO BEHAVIORAL FINGERPRINTS.

Two parties lock eyes from across the room.
The seller is proud, "My business is good."
The buyer is optimistic, "The numbers look great. EBITDA is strong. Let's go!"
The LOI is signed.
The advisors swap emails.
The drafts the first version.
Then comes diligence.
Uh oh, slowly, the clean surface starts to crack.

The EBITDA that looked so strong, starts to look a little shaky.

And then, surprise! Accounts receivable has a big number sitting over ninety days.

And then...tax returns report less income than the internal books.

And then... debt was uncovered. More than anyone expected.

Which raised a hard question: "If EBITDA is really that strong—why is debt needed to fund basic operations?"

Piece by piece, the math wasn't matching the story. Yet both sides were still optimistically charging forward towards closing. The momentum of the deal had taken over and nobody wanted to stop the dance.

But underneath the spreadsheet the real story had cracks. Numbers speak and they do not lie. Sometimes they hint, sometimes they whisper, and sometimes they scream. Your job is to pay attention.

Numbers are the language of business. The difference between a successful business exit and a bankruptcy is the story the numbers tell. When I look at reports, to me the numbers aren't numbers, they are stories. Every entry tells you who ran the business, how they led it, and where the risks are hiding.

> NUMBERS SPEAK AND THEY DO NOT LIE. YOUR JOB IS TO PAY ATTENTION.

This is why every deal, for me, begins with learning to hear the numbers speak before they betray you. Reading financials is not about accuracy—it is about understanding the people, the habits, and the truths that built them.

If you are selling, then your job is to make sure the story you tell the buyer matches the story your numbers tell. When the stories don't match, you are not "finding the missing millions" you are losing them.

If you are buying, then you need to step into the role of an investigator. You have to look beyond the surface. A clean spreadsheet is not proof of a solid business. You must investigate beyond what is seen and known. What would Sherlock Holmes do? (I mean...if he were Holli.) If you do not understand financial statements, get an expert who can. Your job is not to just confirm the seller's story; it is to make sure you can rebuild it yourself. This is a very important distinction. Let me explain.

Most businesses are not built for sale. Their financials

are shaped by years of habits, shortcuts, a string of book-keepers with differing opinions, and decisions that worked for the owner in the moment but may not transfer cleanly to a buyer. Sometimes that mismatch is innocent—they never planned to sell and didn't set up the books for a sale. But sometimes it is intentional—they know what you are looking for and would rather you not see the gaps. Either way, the rule is the same:

Sellers: Prepare your story and your books so they match.

Buyers: Never take EBITDA at face value. Reconstruct it.

And this is where the real detective work begins! Because stories live inside financial statements—not in PowerPoints, not in broker teasers, not in the glossy pitch. Most owners only glance at their P&L once a month, if that. The Balance Sheet? Maybe once a year. The Statement of Cash Flow? Forget it. But these three reports are the only real truth-tellers. And like any good drama, they play their respective roles in the financial story of the business: the P&L and Balance Sheet are the leading love birds, running around together all year (more about that romance later), and right behind them is the Statement of Cash Flow—the paparazzi, publishing the story of where the profit went. The P&L and Balance Sheet whisper their story to each other, but the Cash Flow Statement never holds back! It shouts loudly and tells you exactly what happened to the cash, where it came from, and where it went.

Ever wonder why your business shows a profit but your bank account is empty? The Statement of Cash Flow is the tabloid headline, and it will tell you exactly where the money really went—whether it was eaten up by receivables, piled into inventory, or drained by debt. Profit is opinion. Cash is fact. And the Cash Flow Statement is where the facts come out.

If I could wave my magic wand, every business owner would learn how to read the Cash Flow Statement and receive it in the monthly package from their accountant. Reviewing it is a five-minute exercise that could save millions. If every business owner would do this, fewer businesses would fail in the first five years, and CEOs would be making better decisions. That's not just a rant—this is a strategy for finding the missing millions before they slip away.

If you would like to learn more about how to read and understand the financial statements, check the resources QR code at the end of this book. (Who knows, I might even have a course!) Literally every businessperson needs this information. It's almost shocking to say that at the time of writing this, of all the business deals I have seen over my entire career; I have never once been handed a cash flow statement as part of the package. Not once! Yet it is one of the most valuable tools for understanding the past, present, and future of a business—and it is always missing. (Like the millions.) Sometimes I have recreated it myself. Other times, the story is so clear in the numbers that I do not need to build the report—I can already see where the millions went.

A TRUE STORY: THE BROKER WHO TOLD ME NO

I once tried to buy an accounting firm where the broker offered only a nine-month-old P&L as the basis for a Letter of Intent. No Balance Sheet. When I asked for updated financials and a balance sheet, he flat-out refused. He knew exactly what he was doing: looking for an uneducated buyer willing to take the bait. Well, not me! And not you either. I noped his nope. It was an *accounting firm,* no less!

FINDING THE MISSING MILLIONS: BEHAVIORAL CLUES IN THE NUMBERS

By now you know numbers aren't just math—they are a record of choices, habits, and discipline (or lack of it). So, let's take a look at exactly how this presents itself on paper.

P&L CLUES

- High SG&A: Overstaffed, inefficient, or growth spend that has not paid off.
- Thin margins: Pricing pressure, weak cost control, or poor accounting of expenses.
- Low benefits: Employee retention at risk or benefits never properly recorded.
- Low marketing: Sales tied to the owner instead of a repeatable pipeline.
- High owner compensation: Lifestyle business.
- High office expenses: Personal perks mixed in.
- Low professional fees: Weak accounting oversight, poor accounting controls.

BALANCE SHEET CLUES

- Low cash: Strain, low profitability, owner withdrawals, or poor collection practices.
- High A/R: Uncollectible accounts, inflated revenue, or poor accounting.

- High inventory: Obsolete stock, inflated gross margin, or poor accounting.
- Unchanged liabilities: Unpaid expenses, unrecorded taxes, or poor accounting.
- Strange equity swings: Hidden distributions, personal expenses, or poor accounting.
- Fancy cars: Lifestyle perks, cultural red flags, often hiding in poor accounting.

Notice the pattern? Poor accounting shows up again and again. Where? Mostly on the balance sheet! This is why we need a balance sheet. And here's why that matters: poor accounting doesn't just create messy books—it directly distorts EBITDA. Expenses get tucked away in the wrong place, liabilities are left unrecorded, or QuickBooks "plugs" hold mystery transactions that never get cleaned up. When this happens, the profitability being sold is not the profitability that exists.

Finding the missing millions isn't about one glaring mistake—it's about catching the small lapses in discipline that add up. When you see these clues, you're not just reading numbers. You're uncovering the story of how a business really has been run.

A LOVE STORY (WITH SECRETS & DEAD BODIES)

"Understanding your business is about romance, secrets . . . and dead bodies." I uttered these words to a room full of sharp, ambitious entrepreneurs ready to take the next chapter of their business journey. They expected me to talk numbers. They did *not* expect me to say this. The confusion on their faces was priceless. I think someone almost called security. But the smile on my face? A mile wide. Because once you hear what I have to say about your financials, you'll never un-hear it. And that's the point. I want every business owner to understand this financial romance and never forget it! So, remember: the P&L and the Balance Sheet are in a committed relationship. A full-blown, entangled, ride-or-die kind of romance. You cannot analyze one without the other. Ever. You cannot run the reports on different dates. You cannot make good decisions without seeing them *together.* If your P&L is dated December 31, 2024... then your Balance Sheet better be too. They always show up together. That's the rule. That's the romance. The P&L shouts about how great dinner was last night . . . the Balance Sheet quietly asks whether you can still afford groceries tomorrow.

> POOR ACCOUNTING SHOWS UP AGAIN AND AGAIN. WHERE? MOSTLY ON THE BALANCE SHEET.

The Balance Sheet is the vault of secrets. It quietly holds the stories no one wants to tell—receivables that may never be collected, bills pushed off, credit lines stretched thin, inventory piled high, and liabilities conveniently ignored. And the truth? Most of the errors live here, sitting in plain sight. So, when people say, "the P&L looks good," I always ask: "What did you see on Balance Sheet?"

Sellers: this matters more than you think—review your balance sheet monthly. Buyers: this is where you *must* look. Because the real story? It's told in how these two dance together and if they are out of sync—your deal will be, too. Now, about those "dead bodies" I keep talking about. I said it once in a meeting and I meant it: plural. Where there's one, there's usually more. Here's why. The Balance Sheet (BS) doesn't lie because it *can't.* The BS is such a truth-slaying record. The foundation of the BS and accounting is cash—cash comes in and cash goes out. Cash comes in usually as revenue on the P&L. Cash out goes out as expenses. It *could be* business expenses . . . it *could be* the kid's soccer fees . . . it *could be* repaying the cousin. Who knows? You and I both know that cash payments can be all over the board particularly when personal payments and intercompany transactions get involved. Those mystery payments? They belong on the P&L as expenses—which means *lower* EBITDA, not higher. Normal SMB (small to medium businesses) accounting equals inaccurate EBITDA. When the accountant doesn't know where to record an expense, it gets tucked somewhere on the Balance Sheet. For you QuickBooks users, the software by design has a designated account on the Balance Sheet for "mystery payments." The accountant must fix these monthly. If they don't, your EBITDA is wrong and most likely overstated. Mistakes, old inventory, unfunded 401k plans—these are examples of "dead bodies" that are buried when buyers trust surface-level EBITDA and skip Balance Sheet rigor.

Always assume there are bodies buried until you prove otherwise. If you're buying, never look at a P&L without two Balance Sheets. A single Balance Sheet is just a snapshot at one point in time. To really understand what happened, you need two snapshots—one at the beginning and one at the end. Think of this like watching a movie versus looking at a single photo. If you only look at one photo, you do not know what happened before or after. But with the first and last photo, you can see the change. That change is what reconciles to the P&L. If you're selling? For the love of God, clean up those books! Better *you* find the bodies than a buyer.

A WORD ON ACCOUNTANTS (RED FLAG ALERT):

Most SMBs have accountants who are great at keeping the lights on—paying bills, sending invoices, producing a P&L, hopefully an accurate Balance Sheet, and if you are lucky a Cash Flow Statement. But it's a rare unicorn who can also prepare a company for sale-level diligence. It's not their fault, that's just not what they were hired or trained to do. This isn't about blaming them. It's about understanding that the skills needed to run day-to-day operations are different from the skills needed to prepare financials that withstand a buyer's microscope. You wouldn't call the construction company who built your house when you are ready to sell it, would you? Of course, they know every inch of how it was built. But the skills needed to build a house are different from the skills needed to sell it. In the same way, if you want to maximize your value and avoid expensive surprises when you sell your company, you need external expertise to help you prepare for sale.

Think about this: in the U.S. alone, there's about 2 million accountants. On average, less than 10,000 businesses sell every year. Do you realize how small the likelihood is that your CPA or has any experience at all with the sale of a business? I'll do the math for you: .005%. It's even smaller when you think of people like me who do multiple deals a year. So, unrealistic expectations plus the wrong team equals a recipe for a mess.

STORY: THE MISSING MILLION

I once had a client who hired me to maximize value for a year-end sale. Right from the start, I told him what he did not want to hear, "Your bookkeeper is not qualified to keep these financials in order. If you want maximum value, you need to get her some outside support."

I gave him guidance, I laid out the risks, and I made it clear that inaccurate accounting was going to cost him. But his internal accountant had no idea he was preparing to sell and I was never given direct access to communicate with her.

At year-end, I created a maximized EBITDA. It was clean. It was defensible. It was the best version of his business story. I told him plainly: "Do not let anyone make changes to these books. Not one adjustment. This is the version you take to market."

> YOUR INTERNAL ACCOUNTANT IS NOT TRAINED TO GET YOU THROUGH DILIGENCE GRACEFULLY. YOU CAN BUMBLE YOUR WAY TO A SALE, BUT BUMBLING WILL COST YOU DEARLY.

He took my work to market with a broker and he uploaded the records to the data room himself. Fast forward to when a deal was on the table. When the buyer reviewed the 2024 P&L, it showed $1 million less in revenue than my prepared numbers for the exact same period.

He called me in a panic, "What happened?" I could not tell him. I didn't have access to his bookkeeper to find out. Maybe it was cash vs. accrual. Maybe it was deeper misstatements. It didn't matter at that point. The damage was done. The numbers no longer reconciled, and the inconsistency put the entire sale at risk.

Sellers: you cannot present inadequate accounting to a buyer or bring a digital shoebox of records that don't match and expect to get maximum value. Deals die in the gaps.

HOLLI'S RULE

If the Balance Sheet is wrong, the P&L is wrong. Say it again. Tattoo it if you must. The P&L might look fine. But if the BS has issues? That's the real bs. The earnings you think you are buying may not actually exist.

WHY BOTH SIDES GET IT WRONG

Sellers think: *My numbers reflect my success!* Well . . . probably not. (Don't shoot the messenger.) Remember, most SMBs suffer from inaccurate or incomplete accounting. And even when the books are accurate, they are rarely optimized for a sale. Accounting and diligence are the number one quantifiable reason deals collapse or lose value.

The problems are numerous:

- EBITDA is significantly worse than advertised.
- Reports don't match; numbers don't reconcile.
- The CEO talks about growth and margin but his story doesn't match the actual financial statements.

When any of this happens, the buyer starts seeing more risk—and that means less money for the seller.

Buyers think: *If the EBITDA the seller represents looks good, the business must be solid.*

Your job is to rebuild EBITDA from scratch using both the balance sheet and P&Ls. You look at trends, reconcile accounts, and pressure-test every assumption. Ideally, this should happen before you sign the LOI. Once that LOI is signed, you start spending serious money on diligence, and your leverage drops.

On either side, buyer or seller: your internal accountant

is not trained to get you through diligence gracefully. You can bumble your way to a sale, but bumbling will cost you dearly. Protect your legacy. Bring in an outside expert (like me) to guide you, prepare your numbers, and cultivate your real value.

BOTTOM LINE

Numbers are never just numbers—they are the blueprints for the way a business has been run. If you stop at EBITDA, you are just scratching the surface and you are gambling with ghosts you cannot see. Sellers, make sure your story matches your books *before* you go to market. Buyers, never take numbers at face value—rebuild them yourself.

Because this is where so many "missing millions" hide, I personally developed a practical tool: the EBITDA Normalization Worksheet. It will help you bridge the gap between the story the owner tells and the truth the numbers whisper. In fact, I've created a downloadable M&A "toolbox" for you that you can access via the QR code at the end of the book.

CHAPTER 4

BEFORE YOU DO SH*T, CALCULATE EBITDA

EARNINGS BEFORE INTEREST, TAXES, DEPRECIATION, AND AMORTIZATION

The seller was glowing. "Look at these numbers—EBITDA is through the roof! Best year ever!" The wide-eyed buyer began racing toward an LOI. *Why waste time?* The profit margins looked dreamy, the growth curve flawless, and the deal seemed too good to lose.

The closing date was circled on the calendar, champagne on ice. Spirits were high. Except for one soul—the lone accountant, tucked away in a dimly lit conference room, hunched over a laptop, squinting at spreadsheets that no one else wanted to touch. (Poor thing. Holli has a soft spot for accountants.) The accountant paused, recalculated, and frowned. Something wasn't adding up.

On the shiny P&L, everything gleamed—strong margins, steady growth, a "can't-miss" story sang . . .and danced! But in the background, the Balance Sheet quietly raised its hand. "Excuse me. Look over here," it said politely with a whisper. Reality jarred the accountant—intercompany accounts sat bloated and circular; the kind of shell game that could puff up EBITDA in ways no one would ever catch post-close. Equity swung without explanation, liabilities seemed to vanish, and accounts payable told a story of bills kicked like a can down a dusty road.

Meanwhile, the P&L carried its own skeletons. Rent sat laughably low—an insider's sweetheart deal. And the owner, who practically lived at the office, hadn't taken a salary in years. With the two statements sitting side by side, the "success story" began to look less like a gold mine and more like a mirage.

By the time the questions surfaced, EBITDA was a shadow of its former self. But the wire transfer? Already queued. The seller, meanwhile, was sketching blueprints for his post-sale paradise: a man cave so over the top it had beer taps on demand, three giant screens, and a recliner with cupholders that glowed like a Vegas slot machine. The buyer realized too late that he hadn't just bought a business. He'd financed a fantasy. Behind the P&L, millions had already vanished and he was about to experience the emotional drop of regret after success.

TOUGH LOVE

To be a good seller, you must learn to see through the buyer's eyes. To be a good buyer, you must understand the seller's shoes. Most people think M&A prep is about crunching numbers and shuffling paperwork around at the last minute. Wrong. Preparation is the *soul* of the trans-action. It is where trust is built, leverage is created, and value is either maximized or silently destroyed. Sellers who toss financials across the table like dirty laundry are not just sloppy—they are handing away millions. Buyers who chase a glossy P&L without reconstructing EBITDA are funding lifestyle perks, not profits.

The deal isn't won on closing day—it's won in how prepared you are *before* diligence ever begins.

THE LANGUAGE OF DEALS

Part of the confusion is that buyers and sellers are often speaking different languages. Here's a cheat sheet of what I consider the most important terms and remember, Holli's M&A Survival Glossary is in the back of this book.

- **Seller's Discretionary Earnings** (SDE): EBITDA plus the owner's salary and perks. The Main Street favorite.
- **EBITDA**: Earnings Before Interest, Taxes, Depreciation, and Amortization. The middle-market anchor.
- **Adjusted EBITDA**: EBITDA plus "normalizing" add-backs. The playground for sophisticated buyers.
- **Cash Flow**: The only number that actually matters. This is what's left to service debt, reinvest, and grow.

> LEVERAGE IS CREATED AND VALUE IS EITHER MAXIMIZED OR SILENTLY DESTROYED.

SDE and EBITDA are not cash flow. We will fully unpack this in Chapter 5: "What Can I afford?" but for now, just know these are signals or clues, but they are not the truth. Lock this in: when it comes to M&A, cash flow is the only truth.

SELLERS: CLEAN YOUR HOUSE FOR MAXIMUM VALUE

Sloppy books kill deals, and clean books sell for higher multiples. It is that simple. Do not expect the buyer to normalize expenses for you aka maximize your value. Do not rely on a broker's spreadsheet or a CPA's tax return. Those are not sell-ready books. Buyers will price risk, and sloppiness screams risk.

You should start preparing three to five years before exit if you can. Even with less time, strategic support can accelerate the process. A professional seller prepares a complete data room with reconciled reports, consistent P&Ls, and explanations that match the story. (More on the data room when we get into diligence.)

One client of mine had a strong company but a messy financial story. Within nine months we restructured reporting and cleaned the books. Twelve months after I started, he exited for millions more than expected.

So, what does "cleaning" the books actually look like? Well, it's nothing like cooking them. It looks like presenting the true earnings power of the business by reversing out personal perks—retirement contributions, healthcare premiums, country club dues, vacations, the family car. It means flagging one-time charges, like the M&A advisor you hired or the litigation you had to settle, so they are not mistaken for recurring expenses. It means putting your salary at a market replacement level, not whatever number you happen to pull out. It means correcting rent if your company has been paying your cousin a sweetheart lease. And it means knowing that culture-based bonuses paid year after year are not "one-offs" just because you call them that.

Do this right, and your EBITDA grows—not through smoke and mirrors, but by showing the normalized cash flow that a buyer can actually expect. Do it wrong, and you hand over red flags wrapped in excuses.

When I look at the deals that lose value—it comes back to the type of seller who shows up with tax returns or unclean books. I had a buyer reviewing a company with $6M in top-line revenue. The seller didn't want to alert the bookkeeper, so what did he hand us? Tax returns. While tax returns have a solid place in M&A, it's not at the negotiating table and definitely not when calculating EBITDA.

First, most sellers actually do better when they loop in their accountant—because then they have someone backing them up. Second, I can guarantee two things: handing over tax returns alone, and hiding selling from the accountant, will cost maximum value. And the worst part? The seller had no idea.

Buyers don't pay on tax returns. They pay on normalized EBITDA. And I'll tell you right now—the buyer isn't normalizing your EBITDA. That's your job.

BUYERS: PREPARE BEFORE THE LOI

The worst mistake a buyer can make is walking into an LOI blind waving around the seller's EBITDA like its gospel. It is not. Seller EBITDA is marketing. It is a number built to justify a price, not prove the business can deliver it again tomorrow.

Your job is to rebuild the number from scratch. That means rolling up your sleeves and reverse-engineering EBITDA (or SDE, depending on the deal). Use the normalization worksheet I'm giving you, not the broker's glossy spreadsheet. What you want is reality—not a sales pitch.

Start with the basics:

- 3 years of P&L and balance sheets including trailing twelve months (TTM) if applicable.
- Monthly P&L and balance sheets if available

And then ask yourself: *What doesn't belong?* Bad balance sheet items. One-time charges. Seller perks dressed up as "business expenses." You are not just buying numbers; you are buying their ability to repeat themselves.

Many times, the information contained in a CIM (Confidential Information Memorandum) prepared by a broker or investment banker isn't enough data to prepare an LOI with.

Once you sign an LOI, your leverage is locked. That's why too many buyers overpay—they agree to terms before testing the foundation.

A quick PSA for buyers while we're here: Do not fall in love with a deal. Ever. I know, you think you will not. But it's very common. I have never had a CEO admit that they fell in love and yet, I have seen it more times than I can count. Falling in love makes you blind to the cracks in the story. The only cure is sheer discipline,

> WHEN IT COMES TO M&A, CASH FLOW IS THE ONLY TRUTH.

or a hard loss you don't want to repeat. But by following the principles in this book, deal after deal, you will stay on track! That is how you become the most dangerous buyer in the room: clear-eyed, methodical, and immune to seller sparkle. I used to think all CEOs fell in love at least slightly with their deals—that is until I met Adam Coffey. Adam is the most disciplined CEO I know and the most successful buy-and-build CEO I worked with, logging over $2.5B in exits. If a business doesn't meet his criteria, he walks away. Period. He doesn't try to force it to work because he knows there is always another fish in the sea. He's a rare CEO and I've been blessed to work with him. I talk a lot about discipline in this book and the advice is designed to give you the tools to be as disciplined as Adam.

A COSTLY LOVE STORY

I once worked at a company where the executive team was tasked with growth through acquisition. They found a small company in a location that checked every strategic box. The CEO was thrilled. In fact—he fell in love with the vision. (Not that he would ever admit it.) The CFO was not trained in M&A. And then there was me, an employee/consultant at the time. When I looked at the deal, I kept finding red flags everywhere. Profit was under 10%. The seller was the only salesperson. Operations were in chaos. The team had no leadership, no empowerment. Nothing in the financials resembled their existing business model. But my CEO pushed forward because he had "all the feels." And they closed. After that, it took three years to stabilize. They had to rebuild the sales function from scratch and completely overhauled operations. The seller was long gone. And even after all that investment of time, heart, finances and energy, the location underperformed for years.

LESSON: EMOTION AND STRATEGY CANNOT CO-LEAD A DEAL.

Ok class, let's read that again and say it out loud with me. Now, let's sing it . . . just kidding. The truth is that emotion will always try to sneak into the driver's seat. Remember ATF Syndrome? This is where you have to be careful. Your job is to keep strategy behind the wheel. Every time. Check yourself throughout the process. Run the math. Reread the risks. Ask the hard questions twice.

And if you feel that flutter in your gut—the one that says *I can't wait to make money with this business* watch out!

This is the beginning of the dangerous "Love Connection." Pretend it is indigestion, go back to strategy.

THE DANGER OF FIXER-UPPERS

Turnarounds are not for the faint of heart. Most people cannot do them nor do they know how. It is a special bird who thrives in that kind of chaos.

Here is the quick rule: If you are not a turnaround expert, stay away from businesses running below ~10% EBITDA margin. At that point, you are not buying a business; you are buying a project. And projects? They bleed cash. They suck your time. They demand leadership, capital, patience, and pain tolerance at levels most buyers are not prepared for. Projects will age you faster than raising teenagers.

If you are building an empire with the goal of selling, a fixer-upper will bog you down. It will slow your trajectory, drain your resources, and delay your exit. You cannot scale and repair at the same time without paying a heavy toll. If you think you can "fix it after close," do not. Unless your skill set and capital stack already scream "turnaround" walk away.

THE REALITY OF VALUATION (IN THE WILD)

I say "In the Wild" because that's exactly where I live. I am not a certified valuation expert, and this book is not a lecture hall. You will not find formulas that belong in a CFA exam here. What you will find is the truth of how deals actually get priced when the rubber meets the road. Yes, valuation methods exist—DCF, asset approaches, market comps. They are useful, but they do not belong here, and if you need a formal opinion, you should hire a valuation expert or broker in your industry.

But in the wild? 80–90% of deals run on multiples— and the majority of those are multiples of EBITDA. It is not about elegant models. It is about what the market will pay for your cash flow today. You maximize EBITDA, you apply a multiple, and that is the game. Everything else is noise.

Valuation often comes down to a simple formula:

Revenue × Multiple = MVIC
(Market Value of Invested Capital).

Here is what people actually use:

Multiple	Based On
MVIC / Revenue	Top-line sales
MVIC / EBITDA	Core earnings (the standard)
MVIC / EBIT	Operating earnings
MVIC / SDE	Owner benefit

When the gap between these multiples gets wide, it is a red flag. It usually means there are operational problems, hidden risks, or inconsistent accounting. If you are a seller, buyers will smell blood in the water. If you are a buyer, double-check what story the numbers are really telling you.

In the wild, valuation is not about perfection—it is about negotiation power. Sellers, your job is to maximize normalized adjusted EBITDA and your value. Buyers, your job is to reverse-engineer EBITDA, make sure the "add-backs" actually add up and identify the risks. That's the whole game.

REAL DEAL EXAMPLE: 1X REVENUE VS REALITY

I was representing a buyer for a professional services deal. The seller wanted 1x revenue. When we applied a market EBITDA multiple, the value came in much lower. Why? Because expenses were too high. When revenue multiples and EBITDA multiples diverge widely—that's a red flag that something could be off in operations which requires investigation.

BUYERS: BUILD YOUR BUY BOX

At the height of my buying phase, the CEO and I technically had a "buy box." On paper, it looked fine: industry and geography parameters, revenue ranges, margin targets. But in reality? We ran from one shiny deal to another with no connection to the box we had defined.

We were a West Coast company and one of the worst "detours" was when we somehow found ourselves entertaining a long-time business in Manhattan, New York City. The seller had a boutique service we did not offer and frankly, did not understand. There were a dozen reasons it did not fit—wrong geography, wrong service model, no integration logic, sellers over eighty needing to exit. But at my CEO's behest, we chased it anyway. We wasted time. We wasted money. And most importantly, we distracted ourselves from the strategy that actually worked.

That is the danger of ignoring your buy box. Disciplined buyers stay disciplined and use a Buy Box. They build a clear profile of what they want to buy and, more importantly, what they will not buy—and they stick with it.

Here is a sample Buy Box Criteria—pick what resonates and drop the rest:

- Industry Focus
- Geography
- Revenue Range
- EBITDA
- Business Model (recurring revenue, diverse customers)
- Customer Concentration (no more than 20% per client)
- Key Employee Retention
- Financial Health (consistent profitability, cash flow)
- Growth Potential
- Operational Efficiency
- Risk Factors
- Valuation Multiples
- Integration Potential
- Cultural Alignment
- Due Diligence Readiness
- Seller Motivation

> DISCIPLINED BUYERS
> STAY DISCIPLINED AND
> USE A BUY BOX.

My lesson: shiny deals outside of your buy box will eat your time and potentially your capital. A disciplined buy box keeps you aligned with your strategy and accelerates your path to scale.

THE BOTTOM LINE

The numbers always speak. Your job now is to start listening and stay disciplined with the information you receive.

A downloadable buy box template is available via the QR code at the end of this book.

CHAPTER 5

WHAT CAN I AFFORD?

EBITDA ADD-BACKS, CASH FLOW, AND DEBT COVERAGE

The buyer knew it was tight. The bank signed off on the loan at 1.25x debt coverage (Meaning, you make $1.25, pay $1 to the bank, and only have $0.25 left over in case something goes wrong). The banker smiled. The spreadsheet read, "Approved." Deals were closing every day at this ratio. So why worry?

The first few months hummed along. Payroll cleared. Vendors were paid. Clients mostly paid on time. The seller's revenue forecast wasn't *perfect*, but it was close enough. And then one of their biggest customers called. Their own business was slowing which meant payments would be delayed—but just for a few months. But then . . . two months became four. New contracts the seller had promised as "99% sure" evaporated. Vendor pricing crept up. Interest rates nudged higher and now the buyer was sitting on a $1.05 coverage ratio with only a $.05 cushion, watching his monthly cash flow disappear. The deal had technically worked. Until it didn't—because spreadsheets do not pay debt, cash flow does.

This chapter exists to save you from this kind of pain. Buyers: you are not buying revenue. You are not buying EBITDA. You are buying repeatable, bankable cash flow that funds debt, payroll, and lets you sleep at night. Now, answering the question that is the title of this chapter isn't exactly straight forward. So, sharpen your pencil, fill up your coffee mug and take a nodose if you have to, because this where you are going to need to pay very close attention.

Sellers: in this chapter you will learn how serious buyers test your numbers before they write a check.

Buyers: you will learn how to build a deal you can actually afford—one that will not collapse after closing.

NORMALIZED EBITDA–WHERE THE STORY GETS HONEST

> SPREADSHEETS DO NOT PAY DEBT, CASH FLOW DOES.

Almost every deal conversation starts with EBITDA. It measures core operating profit before financing, tax structure, or non-cash accounting items. But EBITDA is simply your starting point. The seller will present it. The broker will promote it. We start with EBITDA, but we never stop there.

We've already covered that EBITDA is Earnings Before Interest, Taxes, Depreciation, and Amortization. Now, let's talk about normalized EBITDA. When we normalize EBITDA, we add back salaries that won't continue and deduct for any salaries we need to pay post-close. We strip away all the personal, one-time, and non-operating items the seller has layered in over years of ownership, and make adjustments so that EBITDA does not reflect anything "abnormal." When all the abnormal items are removed from the number, what's left is what's considered normal. Hence the term "normalized."

Here are the typical adjustments made when normalizing EBITDA:

Adjustment	What You Are Really Seeing
Personal Expenses	Family salary, retirement plans, country clubs, vacations, private coaching
Owner's Salary	What the current owner actually pays themselves (often inflated or deflated vs. market)
One-Time Legal Fees	Settlements, litigation, M&A services
Professional Services	Personal advisory or consulting buried in operations
Non-Recurring Bonuses	Holiday bonuses, personal "thank you" gifts
Rent Adjustments	If seller owns the real estate
Seller Replacement Salary	Cost of post-close leadership

THE CONSTRUCTION COMPANY WITH A SPIRITUAL P&L

I was helping a seller with a thriving construction firm; strong backlog, great clients and growing bottom line. On the surface, it looked like a premium business. Then I opened the books. Ministry donations were buried under advertising, consulting, and office supplies. Personal coaching expenses showed up in office supplies and in other accounts. You get the picture here. Value was

41

hiding everywhere. Legal settlements were *everywhere*— not just one account. And the same expense categories were handled three different ways across three years of tax returns.

This was not fraud. It was very bad accounting coupled with lifestyle expenses that the bookkeeper didn't know how to handle. This accounting created chaos—and chaos drives down value.

I dug in and started pulling the pieces apart. Line by line, we reclassified expenses, isolated the add-backs, and told the real story behind the numbers. The result? We found $300,000. Every dollar found increased EBITDA and could be multiplied by the market multiple. In this case, $300,000 multiplied by a six multiple equals $1.8M. This is real money.

Messy books are not just a nuisance—they are a signal. To buyers, they whisper: "what else is broken?" And that whisper costs money.

WHEN RED FLAGS SIGNAL FRAUD

Fraud in M&A is more common than most people want to believe. It isn't rare—it shows up in a surprising number of SMB deals. Yet most CEOs are not trained to see it. Why would they be? Running a company requires trusting your team, trusting your numbers, and defaulting to the core belief that people are inherently good.

In M&A, you need to retrain that instinct. Business savvy means maintaining a healthy layer of skepticism. That was drilled into me during my audit career and my CPA exam drove it home as second nature. Once you see fraud, you cannot unsee it.

Fraud does not always show up as theft or something

dramatic. More often, it hides in the subtle things: related-party transactions that don't make sense, aggressive revenue recognition, or numbers that shift just a little too neatly. At first glance, curious transactions look like ordinary red flags or mishaps. But when you tug on the thread, you realize it's more than sloppiness—it's manipulation. Sniffing out fraud isn't about cynicism. It's about protecting value.

Sellers: clean transparency protects your credibility.

Buyers: a healthy level of doubt keeps you from overpaying.

Sellers and buyers both protect the deal when you treat the red flags as signals worth investigating.

Now, let's get back to figuring out what you can afford.

NORMALIZING EBITDA–WHO OWNS THE JOB?

When we talk about normalizing EBITDA, let's be very clear—Sellers: This is *your* job. You are the author of your company's financial story. It is your responsibility to present buyers with a clean, accurate, and defensible version of EBITDA—one that reflects the real, repeatable earning power of your business once you exit. You do this by identifying and documenting legitimate add-backs:

- Personal expenses (family salary, cars, country club, vacations, etc.)
- One-time legal or consulting fees
- Rent adjustments if you own the building
- Seller replacement salary (cost to replace your role post-close)
- Non-recurring charges (litigation, one-off bonuses, special projects)

The more transparent, consistent, and well-documented your adjustments are, the stronger your position becomes. Clean books attract strong multiples.

Buyers: Your job is <u>not</u> to build add-backs for the seller. Your job is to test, validate, and pressure-check the seller's normalization claims. You are reading the story the seller has written and making sure the facts hold up under scrutiny. When you review a seller's normalized EBITDA, your checklist becomes:

- Is this truly non-recurring? Or will I need to pay it post close?
- Are there intercompany or related party transactions in the books?
- Is there proper documentation? Can I verify the claim?
- Do the adjustments reflect my post-close reality?
- Are there expenses that should not have been added back?
- Are any recurring expenses being disguised as "one-time"?

A NOTE ON BUYER SYNERGIES

Like couples newly dating, excited buyers often start mentally crediting their future synergies to the seller just to make the price work. For example, a buyer might rationalize, "We'll merge back-office functions, so we can afford to pay more now." No. Those cost savings or revenue lifts are *yours*, not the sellers. If you are rationalizing how to make it work, just don't. You can't make a deal based on hope for future execution, because reality is based on past performance. Pay for the business as it stands today, not for what you hope to transform it into tomorrow. Discipline means valuing what is, not what might be.

AGGRESSIVE OR STRATEGIC?

I was helping a seller prepare his business for market. He was confident—maybe a little too confident. He insisted on adding back his entire salary. His reasoning? "My second-in-command can take over. I won't need to be replaced."

Then came the recruiting fees. Another add-back. "That was a mistake," he said. "We won't use recruiters again. They don't work for our model."

At first glance, it was aggressive accounting. But digging a little deeper clearly revealed what he was really trying to show: the strength of his internal team. And that's what buyers want to see—that the business is not just about the founder and that there is a bench—knowing that operations won't fall apart the day after close.

> PAY FOR THE BUSINESS AS IT STANDS TODAY, NOT FOR WHAT YOU HOPE TO TRANSFORM IT INTO TOMORROW.

But here's the thing: claiming that someone can step up isn't the same as proving it. Buyers want evidence. Has that second-in-command led before? Are they respected by the team? Do they even *want* the top job? And are you really prepared to scale without ever hiring externally again? Aggressive add-backs are a signal—sometimes of risk, sometimes of value.

EBITDA NORMALIZATION WALKTHROUGH

Let's run an example of calculating EBITDA:

- Reported EBITDA: $1,000,000
- Add-backs for personal expenses: $150,000
- One-time legal: $50,000
- Rent add-back: $75,000 (rent can be an add-back or a deduct depending on whether or not rent is at fair market value)
- Seller replacement salary adjustment: -$125,000

Normalized EBITDA: $1,000,000 + $150,000 + $50,000 + $75,000 - $125,000 = $1,150,000

To calculate the Enterprise Value, apply the market multiple. In our example, we are using 4x: $1,150,000 x 4 = $4,600,000

Missing millions anyone? Surprise! Here they are!

CAPEX: THE BUYER'S BLIND SPOT

Now, here's where many first-time buyers take their hardest hit: EBITDA ignores the future. You can look at a business today and think the numbers are rock-solid, only to find out tomorrow that those same numbers are hiding a ticking time bomb. Trucks don't run forever. Software becomes obsolete. Equipment wears down. If major replacements or upgrades are coming due, those future expenses are not sitting in EBITDA. However, they will be reducing your cash after you buy, and sometimes immediately. These expenses are known as CapEx or Capital Expenditures. To recap CapEx, this refers to the money a business spends to acquire, maintain, or upgrade long-term assets—things that will be used for more than a year like buildings or real estate, machinery and equipment, vehicles, technology infrastructure, etc.

THE LANDLORD SURPRISE

We had just closed on a new location—another jewel in our growing empire. I was the buyer, working closely with my CEO and we had paid a fair multiple on EBITDA. Everything looked clean. Solid team, strong margins, good location.

As is often the case, the seller personally owned the building that housed the business. It was separate from what we purchased. During diligence, we reviewed the lease. It had about nine months remaining. At the time, renewing seemed like a formality—we trusted the relationship and the seller gave us verbal assurance it would not be an issue. But we made a critical mistake: we did not secure formal renewal rights or negotiate a new lease before closing.

Shortly after the deal closed, the seller changed course. He decided to sell the building. Because we had no renewal option in place, we no longer had a legal right to stay. We were forced to vacate. What followed was months of operational disruption, over $100,000 in moving costs, and a long, expensive build-out in a new facility with significantly higher rent.

We had overlooked a crucial piece of real estate diligence and it cost us. On paper, EBITDA held steady. But in reality, cash flow took a serious hit. The higher rent, the build-out costs, the unexpected relocation—none of it showed up in the multiple we paid, but surprise! All of it showed up in the bank account. That is the difference between EBITDA and cash flow. One is a metric, the other is the actual money you use to pay your team, fund growth, and survive disruption. Before you close, make sure you understand the capital investments required to keep the business running—not just the earnings it previously generated.

Also, protect your future operating footprint as carefully as you protect your P&L. A lease without renewal rights can turn into a silent cashflow destroyer.

> THE DIFFERENCE BETWEEN EBITDA AND CASH FLOW: ONE IS A METRIC, THE OTHER IS THE ACTUAL MONEY YOU USE TO PAY YOUR TEAM, FUND GROWTH, AND SURVIVE DISRUPTION.

CAPEX BEST PRACTICES

Capital expenditures can be one of the most overlooked pieces of valuation for new buyers and sellers. The disciplined buyer (and the smart seller) dig into the history and the future of CapEx. Start by looking back at least three years of spending and compare it to industry norms. Patterns matter. Was investment steady, or were assets starved? The disciplined seller already has considered CapEx and it is a part of the story.

Then ask the hard questions: Which assets are nearing the end of their useful life? Has maintenance been deferred, waiting for "the next owner" to deal with it? Are new regulations or technologies going to demand upgrades you haven't budgeted for? And don't forget the hidden landmines—leases and facilities that could carry big move-out costs, remediation, or buildouts once the ink is dry.

Finally, look forward. Forecast realistic future CapEx, not only what the seller hands you, but what truly is required to keep revenue flowing and operations healthy. Buyers who skip this step end up with "surprise" investments that eat the very cash flow they thought would cover debt. Sellers who address it early signal discipline and reduce the "haircut" buyers often take to cover the unknowns.

Bottom line:
CapEx is not a footnote. It is a silent valuation lever—
and that's no cap!

IMPACT OF CAPEX ON EBITDA– HOW DISCIPLINED BUYERS THINK

On paper, EBITDA can look like a king-sized number. A company showing $1.15 million in normalized EBITDA at a 4× multiple is valued at $4.6 million. But here's the catch: this business requires $300,000 of capital expenditures every year just to keep the lights on—replacing trucks, updating systems, maintaining equipment. This was not optional, it was survival.

EBITDA ignores that reality. Buyers do not. They translate EBITDA into sustainable, bankable cash flow. Subtract the $300,000 in recurring CapEx, and true cash flow looks more like $850,000. Apply the same 4× multiple, and suddenly the valuation falls closer to $3.4 million—that's a $1.2 million discrepancy in a single calculation. That is the discipline: buyers do not pay for theoretical earnings power; they pay for cash they can actually use.

Smart buyers know CapEx can be fuzzy. So, they press:

• Is it *sustaining* CapEx—needed to just to keep the wheels turning; or *growth* CapEx—used to unlock future revenue? Unless proven otherwise, assume sustaining for most.

- Is it recurring or lumpy? A heavy year might look scary, but buyers will average CapEx over a cycle.
- How does it stack up against peers? If CapEx as a percentage of revenue is high, it becomes a pricing lever.
- What about taxes? Depreciation from CapEx creates a tax shield, meaning the cash drain is not always dollar-for-dollar.

And here's the big one: when sellers underinvest for years, buyers: YOU will inherit the bill. Deferred maintenance, aging equipment, outdated systems—the next owner has to pay for all of it. If you are a buyer, you must decide how to reflect that risk in the price, because disciplined buyers always will.

But sellers are not without rationale—and this is where you can lean in.

- Growth, not patchwork: "This spend is expanding capacity, not just fixing leaks."
- Lumpy, not recurring: "We already made the heavy investments. The future run rate will normalize."
- Tax efficiency: "Yes, it is cash out, but it drives depreciation and lowers taxable income."
- Industry norms: "This is not mismanagement—it is the cost of doing business at scale."

EBITDA AND SDE ARE NOT CASH FLOW

SDE—Seller's Discretionary Earnings—is often the starting point for valuing the smallest businesses. Think "Main Street" deals: family-owned shops, lifestyle businesses, owner-operator companies. It is meant to capture all the benefit an owner pulls out of the business—salary, perks, personal expenses, even the car lease that never leaves the driveway. Buyers of very small businesses (often first-time owners or individual operators) want to know: *If I step into your shoes, how much cash can I put in my pocket?* That's what SDE tries to answer.

EBITDA, on the other hand, is the language of middle-market and larger deals. Private equity, institutional buyers, and strategic acquirers use it because it strips away the noise of individual owner perks and focuses on operating performance. Multiples are usually applied to EBITDA, not SDE, once a business is big enough to stand on its own, independent of the founder's lifestyle.

Neither SDE nor EBITDA equals true, bankable cash flow. You don't pay your bank note with EBITDA. You don't fund growth, taxes, or new hires with SDE. What you are really buying in any deal is repeatable, durable, *cash flow*.

Cash flow has to cover:

- Debt service—your loan payments will not wait
- Growth capital—expansion, new hires, new equipment
- Taxes—ignored at your peril
- Working capital—that never-ending cycle of receivables, payables, and inventory
- Surprises—because there are always surprises

SDE and EBITDA are simply steppingstones—convenient metrics to compare businesses and apply multiples. But if you stop there, you risk overpaying for numbers that look good on paper but cannot actually support the business in practice. The real test is cash flow. Always. And yes, working capital deserves its own spotlight—it is messy, misunderstood, and often the silent deal-killer.

That's why it has its own chapter later on in this book. But for now, let's have a Mock-Tale. . .

PAIN AT THE PUMP

You've finally done it—you bought your dream car. Yes, that one. The sleek machine you've been eyeing for years. You've mapped out a road trip to your dream destination, and in the purchase agreement, the seller promised to include "enough gas to get you there."

It seems straight forward but the parameters weren't clearly defined. You think it'll take ten gallons to make the trip. But when you tell that to the seller, he swears three will do the trick. Who's right? Doesn't matter—a kerfuffle ensues. Each side digs their heals in. And that, my friend, is working capital.

Now let's put this into deal context. Say you're buying an accounting firm in November. On paper, it looks great. But here's the catch: it's running on fumes this time of year. Zero working capital. Because of the seasonality of the business, you need a full tank of working capital—enough "gas" to carry operations until March when the busy season kicks in.

If the seller doesn't load the tank before you drive off the lot, you'll be stuck finding fuel and a second loan just to keep the engine running. And suddenly that "good deal" costs you millions more after close.

That's why working capital isn't just a line on a balance sheet. It's the gas in the tank. And if you don't negotiate it right, you'll sputter out on the side of the road before you ever hit the highway. Don't worry, we will talk more about working capital in just a bit.

THE BUYER'S CASH FLOW WATERFALL

Ok class, great work so far! We are this much closer to answering our question of the chapter. Now, let's put it all together and do a quick review of what is known collectively as the Buyer's Cash Flow Waterfall—because the movement of money is structured like water cascading down different tiers. AND very soon, you will be able to calculate what you can actually afford.

It always starts the same way—with the number everyone loves to brag about: EBITDA. That headline figure gets splashed across broker decks and whispered over golf courses like its gospel. But by now you know, EBITDA is not the truth, it's just the opening act. Step one is normalization, where you strip away the gloss. Seller's family car on the books? Gone. Above-market

> WHAT YOU ARE REALLY BUYING IN ANY DEAL IS REPEATABLE, DURABLE, *CASH FLOW*.

rent to a cousin's LLC? Corrected. One-time lawsuit? Out. Normalization pulls EBITDA closer to reality.

Step two is CapEx. This is the part new buyers often stumble on but not my readers! You already know that EBITDA ignores what it actually costs to keep a business alive. Trucks wear out. Servers crash. Equipment fails. That shiny EBITDA line doesn't fix the roof—you do. Sustaining CapEx is real cash out the door, and disciplined buyers subtract it before they ever start thinking about value.

Step three is working capital—At closing, the seller usually delivers normalized working capital—which is the fuel in your tank. That is part of the purchase price. But if the business consumes more working capital than what is delivered (common in growth situations), that short-fall reduces the cash available to you. That is why in the

Buyer's Waterfall we show potential additional working capital needs.

Buyer's Cash Flow Waterfall

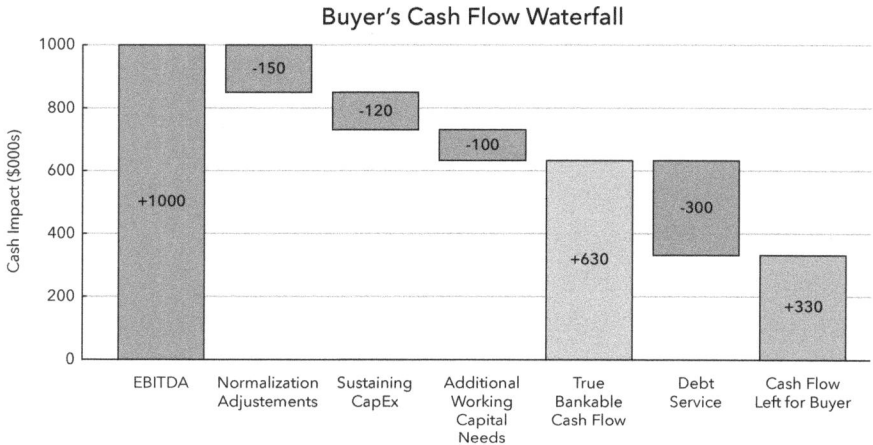

Buyer's Cash Flow Waterfall

BUILDING YOUR DEAL STACK

Now that you understand how cash flow cascades down the waterfall, the next question is: *How do you actually plan to pay for the business?* This is where the capital stack comes in. Deals are rarely funded with a single check—they are built in layers, each with its own role and risk.

- Seller's Note: Often carrying below-market interest or even interest-only payments for a time, a seller's note is the cheapest and most flexible debt you will find. It also keeps the seller tied to your success because they only get fully paid if the business continues to perform.
- Rollover Equity: Instead of cashing out 100%, the seller may "roll" some of their equity into your new entity. For you, this lowers the cash you need at close. For

them, it is a chance to ride the upside of your growth. Think of it as alignment money.

• Your Equity (Cash In): This is your skin in the game. Lenders, sellers, and investors all look for it. It proves belief.

• Debt Financing: Whatever is left must be financed. Many first-time buyers turn to the SBA, while others seek commercial loans. Debt is the last piece of the stack— and the most unforgiving.

When you add these layers together, you arrive at the full picture of how the deal is paid for. This capital stack sits side by side with your waterfall. One shows what the business produces in cash; the other shows how you're funding the purchase. Together, they answer the real question: *Can I afford this deal?*

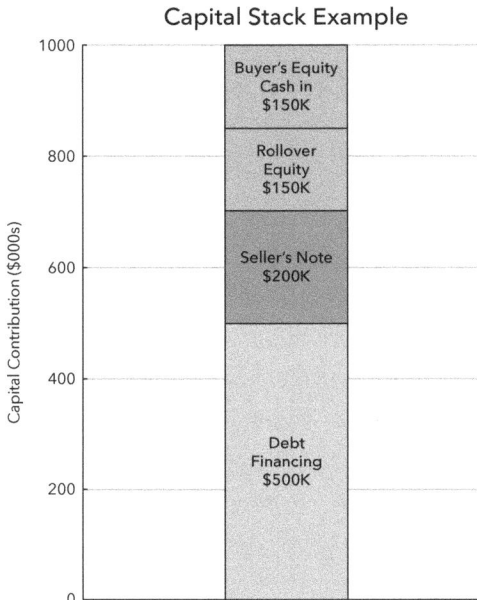

Capital Stack Example

THE DEBT COVERAGE TEST–THE RULE OF 2

Now, let's put the deal through a reality check. This is where true bankable cash flow collides with the cold math of paying the bank every month. Think of it as a "stress test" for your deal. If the business can't comfortably cover its debt payments, the deal doesn't work.

Here is an example:

Debt Service Coverage Ratio = True Bankable Cash Flow ÷ Debt Payments example:

- True Cash Flow = $1.4M
- Enterprise Value = $6.3M (4.5x multiple)
- Debt Financing: $4M over 10 years at 10%
- Buyer Equity: $1M
- Seller Note: $1.3M interest only at 7%

Annual Debt Payments:

- Bank payment = $634K
- Seller note interest = $91K
- Total debt payment = $725K

Debt Service Coverage Ratio (true cash flow/total debt payments): $1.4M ÷ $725K = 1.93x

That's almost at my recommended "Rule of 2." What does that mean? It means I want at least two dollars of true, bankable cash flow for every one dollar of debt service —giving you enough coverage to confortably make debt payments and still have a healthy buffer. *You are almost at my recommended safety level of 2.0 and probably close enough depending on your personal risk profile.*

WHY THE RULE OF 2 WHEN THE BANKS ARE OKAY WITH 1.25X?

The only thing you can predict with confidence in business ownership is that unpredictable things will happen. And when they do, you will need cash, and more than you think. If a key customer walks away or collections slow or vendors raise prices, wages spike or technology fails, or the economy shifts. Any one of these can hit your cash flow hard. Two or three at the same time? That can sink you.

That's why I encourage every buyer to target a 2.0x debt service coverage ratio. That means for every dollar of debt you owe, you want two dollars of real, bankable cash flow—one dollar to make the bank payment, and another dollar to protect yourself, pay yourself, and keep the business running no matter what.

> EBITDA IS JUST A STARTING POINT. IT TELLS YOU WHAT THE BUSINESS HAS EARNED HISTORICALLY. THE REAL TEST IS KNOWING WHAT IT CAN EARN GOING FORWARD.

Yes, many lenders will only require 1.25x coverage. That may be fine for them because they get paid first and they don't have to keep the business alive. But for you, that leaves just twenty-five cents on the dollar for everything else. That is not a cushion; it is a dangerous way to operate.

Do not enter into deals that leave you financially exposed.

THE BOTTOM LINE

EBITDA is just a starting point. It tells you what the business has earned historically. But the real test is what the business can earn and afford going forward. That is where debt coverage comes in. Plenty of deals look good on a spreadsheet. But when payments start and margins tighten, discipline is what keeps you out of trouble. Again, you are not buying a number, you are buying the ability for cash flow to show up again next month, next quarter, and next year.

A downloadable EBITDA Normalization & Debt Coverage Calculator is available via the QR code at the end of this book.

CHAPTER 6

THE VALUE CHESSBOARD

DELIBERATELY SETTING YOURSELF UP FOR THE WIN

The chess grandmaster sat in the corner of a private club, the fireplace crackling, casting a soft glow across the board. Dark wood. Low voices. Glasses clinking under the hush of deal talk. But his eyes never left the game. He carried a dozen variations in his head—seeing not just the next move, but the chain of moves that could follow, branching like rivers across the board.

Across from him sat a young executive. Fresh off his first acquisition. Grinning. Confident. Ready to "crush integration."

The grandmaster moved a knight. Quiet. Precise. Deadly.

The executive leaned in with a smile, already reaching for his queen. He thought the game was his. "Check," he said proudly.

But the grandmaster saw what the young executive didn't: every flashy move is only as strong as the chain of moves behind it.

The grandmaster, anticipating the young executive's move, wasted no time to respond with his. "Checkmate" said the grandmaster softly.

The young executive fell back into his leather chesterfield chair, staring at the board in disbelief. The grandmaster sipped his old fashioned and smiled.

Like the game of chess, in M&A, it's not the move you make—it's the moves you set into motion.

BUILDING VALUE

M&A is never just about the numbers. It is about the positioning, the timing, the sequence of moves that make winning possible. In other words, an M&D deal is a chessboard. And no, you do not have to know chess to follow me here. What matters is understanding that each piece on the board has a role to play in adding value, and that the game is often won or lost in the strategy—long before anyone says "checkmate."

> BUSINESS VALUE IS NOT MAGIC, IT IS A SERIES OF DELIBERATE MOVES PLAYED YEARS IN ADVANCE.

Business value is not magic—it is a series of deliberate moves played years in advance.

Whether you are selling tomorrow or buying today the "pieces" you have on your board and the way you position them determine your future.

In M&A, most sellers think the game is all about the king—EBITDA, and most buyers think it is all about price. But the real game is more sophisticated. It is the rook of leadership strength, guarding the business when the owner exits. It is the bishop of disciplined systems, cutting diagonally through complexity. It is the knights of diverse revenue, leaping past single points of failure. It is the pawns—your brand, your customer relationships, your intellectual property—advancing slowly, often overlooked, but capable of deciding the entire match. And the compelling Queen committed to strategic growth.

A seller who prepares their board with precision, commands a higher multiple. A buyer who sees beyond

EBITDA acquires a company that integrates smoothly and scales gracefully.

Now, let's have some fun breaking down the board, piece by piece, finding missing millions so you can make every move count and maximize the success of the transaction.

WHY VALUE ISN'T JUST EBITDA

Everyone loves the king. In M&A, that king is EBITDA. It's big, it's loud, and it tends to get all the attention. But no grandmaster wins on the king alone. When buyers focus only on EBITDA, they risk overpaying for a shaky structure. When sellers only polish EBITDA, they leave money on the table—because smart buyers know to look at the whole board. Value is a composite. A story in motion. A fortress built on many pieces: team leadership bench, systems discipline, customer concentration, recurring revenue, brand story, even your headquarters.

Buyers: These "pieces" reduce your future headaches, protect your cash flow, and create scalability.

Sellers: Let's make you irresistible—these same pieces help you command the premium you dream about.

THE ROOK: YOUR TEAM/BACKLINE

For sellers, your team is your rook—the silent protector on your chessboard. When you can prove that your business runs without you, your value rises. A strong second-in-command bench, a clear succession plan, and leaders who can operate independently of the founder signal stability and scalability. This shows buyers that the business is a well-built machine, not a one-person performance.

For buyers, a business that functions without its founder

in the day-to-day typically commands a premium—and for good reason. It reduces transition risk, speeds integration, and frees you to focus on growth instead of firefighting. Even if you are acquiring a lifestyle business or structuring an earnout so the seller can build depth over time, you will always be in a stronger position when the team is already in place. Value increases when the rook is standing guard.

THE BISHOPS: SYSTEMS & PROCESSES

For sellers, system discipline is your bishop—the piece that cuts diagonally through chaos. In chess, the bishop moves with precision, quietly shaping the board in ways that less disciplined players overlook. In business, disciplined operating systems do the same. They cut through the noise, reduce errors, and give buyers confidence that what they see in diligence will match what they experience post-close. Sloppy, or undocumented processes do the opposite. They create friction, raise questions, and force buyers to imagine the worst. If you cannot clearly show how sales are generated, how services are delivered, how cash is managed, or how compliance is maintained, you are signaling risk—and risk erodes value.

Buyers, take note: strong operating systems are not just about efficiency; they are about predictability. A company with clean financials, documented operations, and a strategic plan is far more likely to deliver the EBITDA you are paying for. You can integrate it faster, manage it more easily, and scale it with less disruption.

For sellers, the winning moves are clear: document your core processes—sales, service delivery, finance, HR. Implement consistent financial reporting with accurate books, timely monthly closes, and cash flow forecasting.

Tighten your compliance, HR, and legal housekeeping. Have a strategic plan with measurable goals. When you can demonstrate this kind of discipline, your bishop becomes one of the most powerful pieces on your board—and buyers will pay for the advantage it brings.

THE KNIGHTS: REVENUE AND CUSTOMER DIVERSITY

In chess, knights are the unpredictable movers. They leap over pieces, bypass obstacles, and land where others cannot. In business, your revenue strategy should be just as agile—able to avoid traps and recover quickly from threats.

For sellers, the most dangerous trap is concentration risk—when too much of your revenue depends on a single customer, a single product, or a single market. A buyer looking at a company with 50% of revenue tied to one client is not thinking about opportunity; they are calculating risk. And risk drags your valuation down. The reality is, no matter how loyal you believe that client is, a change in their leadership, budget, or priorities can wipe out half your revenue overnight.

Knights win by having multiple paths to the same goal. In business, that means diversifying your customer base, building recurring or contracted revenue streams, and strengthening your pricing power so you are not forced into unnecessary discounts. Each of these "moves" gives you options, and in M&A, options are leverage.

For buyers, diverse revenue is more than just a nice-to-have; it is post-close insurance! Without it, the "big client" you are counting on might vanish before you even finish celebrating the deal. With it, you are buying a business that can take a hit and keep moving forward, just like a knight maneuvering around the board with confidence.

THE PAWNS: INTANGIBLES & BRAND EQUITY

In chess, the pawns are often overlooked—slow, limited in movement, seemingly expendable. But in the hands of a skilled player, they can march across the board, transform into queens, and shift the power of the entire game.

In business, your pawns are the intangible assets that rarely show up on the balance sheet—your brand reputation, your company culture, your customer experience. These may seem like small players compared to hard assets or EBITDA, but they carry the power to unlock enormous value when nurtured and played properly.

A seller who invests in these assets is playing the long game. Every five-star review, every positive mention in the community, every touchpoint that leaves a customer feeling valued—these are pawns inching forward. Marketing assets, clean and robust CRM data, a compelling mission, and a well-told brand story are all pieces that reinforce the company's positioning in the market. Even something as tangible as a polished, thoughtfully designed headquarters can signal credibility and reinforce your promise to clients and employees alike. To a buyer, these intangibles are not just "nice to have," they are hidden engines of growth. They open doors, reduce the cost of acquiring new customers, and make employees and clients stickier. If leveraged well post-close, these quiet pawns can become the queens that drive expansion and long-term success.

THE QUEEN: STRATEGIC GROWTH ENGINE

If EBITDA is the king (fragile but central), the queen is the force multiplier—the element of your business that can shift the entire board in one move. The queen represents scalable growth drivers that unlock disproportionate value:

- Technology or Proprietary IP → software, AI, or a unique platform that lets you leapfrog competitors.
- Channel Access / Distribution Power → a sales engine, exclusive contracts, or customer acquisition strategy that accelerates growth.
- Brand Equity with Reach → not just reputation (your pawns already carry that) but the ability to turn reputation into rapid expansion.
- Culture & Talent Magnetism → the type of culture or leadership brand that attracts top talent and keeps the flywheel turning.

> INTANGIBLE ASSETS RARELY SHOW UP ON THE BALANCE SHEET. THEY CARRY THE POWER TO UNLOCK ENORMOUS VALUE WHEN NURTURED PROPERLY.

Unlike the rook, bishop, or knight—each important but limited in scope; the queen moves in every direction. She's the business's unfair advantage; the asset that both protects the king (EBITDA) and drives expansion.

THE KING: EBITDA

In M&A, the king of the chessboard is EBITDA—powerful, central, and the piece everyone watches. As long as the king is standing, the game is still in play. But in chess, the king is fragile on his own. A king never wins a game by himself. His power only holds if the other pieces are protecting him. Leadership depth, disciplined systems, diversified revenue, and brand strength are the rook, bishop, knight, pawns, and queen that keep the king—EBITDA—standing. Without them, EBITDA is exposed—and the deal that looks strong on paper can collapse under real-world pressure.

Buyers pay multiples on EBITDA because it represents the engine of future cash flow. But smart buyers do not stop there. They scan the rest of the board. Can the business run without the founder? Do the systems support scale? Is revenue concentrated or diversified? Does the brand actually carry weight with customers? If those answers come back weak, the king topples and the multiple falls with him. It's "game over" at that point!

THE VALUE CHESSBOARD SUMMARY

♔ King—EBITDA
The center of the board. Buyers value your company first and foremost on EBITDA.

♕ Queen—Strategic Growth Drivers
Your most powerful lever: technology, distribution, brand reach, or culture that unlocks disproportionate growth.

♖ Rooks—Leadership Bench
The protectors. A strong team and succession plan show buyers the business runs without you.

♗ Bishops—Disciplined Systems

Cut across the board. Documented processes, accurate books, compliance, forecasting and a strategic plan prove scalability.

♘ Knights—Diverse Revenue

Agile and resilient. No concentration risk, recurring contracts, and pricing power create freedom of movement.

♙ Pawns—Brand & Relationships

Small moves, big compounding value. Customer loyalty, reviews, IP, and community reputation build credibility.

BUYERS: WHY THIS MATTERS TO YOU

When you acquire a business, you are not simply buying a set of numbers on a spreadsheet. You are buying the entire system that produced those numbers—every piece on the chessboard. If the board is messy, with missing or weak pieces, you are inheriting higher risk, potential integration headaches, and expensive post-close clean-up.

This is where the missing millions hide. If you pay a premium for a broken board, you are buying problems instead of performance. By staying disciplined, you capture value at the table, not after the fact. This is how buyers maximize value and minimize regret.

A disciplined chessboard, on the other hand, means reduced risk, smoother integration, and a better return on your investment. The stronger your position on the chessboard, the more upside you can capture without the risk of paying a multiple for nothing more than hope.

SELLERS: WHY THIS MATTERS TO YOU

Buyers reward businesses that are de-risked and future ready. They pay more for clean, well-run companies where the chessboard is set up for success after the owner leaves. When your business demonstrates stability, systems, and growth potential, you move from hoping for a premium to commanding one. This is how you unlock the missing millions—by setting up the board so buyers see value, not risk. The effect is powerful. This creates competitive tension in the market because multiple buyers will chase a business that is well-positioned and we all know—competition drives price!

> IF YOU PAY A PREMIUM FOR A BROKEN BOARD, YOU ARE BUYING PROBLEMS INSTEAD OF PERFORMANCE.

In M&A, a strong chessboard is not just a negotiating advantage, it is the foundation of maximizing value, minimizing regret, and getting paid for what you have actually built.

YOUR VALUE CHESSBOARD CHECKLIST

Think of this as your quick scan before you make your next move:

- Leadership Bench: Do you have strong, empowered leaders who can run the business without you?
- Systems: Are your processes documented, repeatable, and followed consistently?
- Financials: Are your accounting records accurate, timely, and based on principles buyers trust?
- Revenue: Is your customer base diversified and defensible, with recurring or contracted streams?

- Brand & Culture: Are your brand assets, reputation, and culture clear, strong, and transferable?
- Scalable growth drivers: Technology, AI, culture and brand expansion?
- EBITDA: Is your EBITDA both healthy and sustainable, backed by a credible story that proves it will continue?

In M&A, the chessboard you present whether as a buyer evaluating a deal or a seller preparing for one, determines whether you are playing for a quick checkmate or a long, painful defense. A well-prepared board gives you control, leverage, and the ability to play on your terms.

THE BOTTOM LINE

Value is not a single number, it's a chessboard of strategic moves. Whether you're selling in five years or buying next quarter, you are playing this game already. Get your pieces in place. Strengthen your position. Reduce risk. Then, when the time comes, you will not just win—you will win with maximum value by finding the missing millions.

Remember, every deal carries risk, but the goal is always the same—maximize value and minimize regret.

CHAPTER 7

PE–TURNING TRICKS

HOW THE PROS FIND MILLIONS OVERNIGHT–AND YOU CAN, TOO!

The deal closed late on a Friday. The seller's team clinked champagne glasses, exhausted but triumphant. Years of blood, sweat, and payroll met their finish line. The buyer's team flew home, binders full of diligence notes stamped *complete.*

By Monday morning, nothing looked different inside the business. The same staff showed up at the same desks. The same customers called in. The same trucks rolled out of the lot. But in a glass tower far away, the private equity team updated their model. Overnight, the company they had just bought is now worth millions more. On paper. Without adding a single dollar of revenue or changing a single thing about the functionality of the business.

The seller had no idea. Worse—he would never see it. What happened? Where did this money come from . . . literally overnight? *Was this a trick? Was it fraud?* The answer is no. No trick. No smoke and mirrors. No fraud.

Surprise! This is the magic of proper accounting.

Private equity firms understand how to leverage proper accounting to create millions of dollars in value, and by the end of this chapter you will, too.

Now, let's talk about GAAP. No, this isn't where you buy jeans. GAAP stands for Generally Accepted Accounting Principles (or for my international readers anytime I reference GAAP think IFRS (International Financial Reporting

Standards) which has similar benefits to GAAP. This dull, boring acronym is completely ignored by most small-business owners; however, it is the scalpel private equity wields to create millions of dollars in value.

THE GAAP WHISPERER

I was tapped for this trick early in my career. Back then, I was an auditor at a CPA firm. One of my clients was a fast-growing manufacturing company whose CEO was preparing to sell. He plucked me out of public accounting and dropped me straight into the deal. My assignment? Use every GAAP lever I knew to maximize EBITDA. So, I did. This was not fraud. It was GAAP. And at that point, I was considered a GAAP expert.

Anyone who really knows accounting understands that GAAP is not at all black and white. In fact, it is many shades of grey and in those grey areas, millions of dollars can appear or disappear.

So, I went to work on the numbers. Nothing in the factory changed. The same trucks rolled out. The same workers clocked in. But on paper, the company was instantly more profitable, more stable, and more valuable. Cha ching!

This was my initiation into the world of M&A. I learned that value can be created or destroyed without ever touching operations. All it takes is the right accounting lens. And here is what still shocks me all these years later: in most M&A rooms, no one talks about this! However, strategic and PE buyers know the real game is in the magic of proper accounting.

THE TRICK NOBODY TALKS ABOUT

GAAP. This is where the game splits wide open. Small and mid-sized businesses almost always set up and run their books for taxes. They operate with one strategy in mind: keep taxable income low. Expense everything. Minimize what Uncle Sam sees. They set up and run their books for *taxes*. In contrast, strategic buyers and private equity set up and run their books for *value*. In fact, they assume two sets of books—one for the IRS, one for investors. (Yes, you can do that.) And they understand that accounting isn't just compliance. It's positioning. It's leverage. It's where the missing millions hide. P.E. doesn't just buy your company; they buy your accounting. Then they "fix" it. On top of this,

> VALUE CAN BE CREATED OR DESTROYED WITHOUT EVER TOUCHING OPERATIONS.

they have super ninja accounting moves that you do not know about. The day after close, the numbers tell a different story—richer, cleaner, investor-ready. The business looks more valuable, not because anything changed, but because it's written in the right business language which is . . . surprise! Generally Accepted Accounting Principles yes, boring GAAP. And in bigger companies? This actually isn't a trick—it's expected. Two sets of books: tax and GAAP are the norm.

THE NINJA TRICKS THEY USE

Here is a list of common "tricks" used every day by big companies and private equity. None of these are shady. They're standard practice, just invisible to most SMB owners.

- **First Trick isn't Really a Trick**

If your accounting is wrong and the buyer can benefit, you will never know.

- **Cash vs. Accrual Accounting**

If your books are on cash basis and accrual would recognize more revenue, the buyer simply flips the method. *Bam. More EBITDA. Nothing else changes.* Growing businesses almost always show better numbers on accrual.

- **Capitalization vs. Expensing**

That AI platform you built? The ERP system you rolled out? The rebrand you launched? Your CPA probably expensed it to save you taxes this year. Under GAAP, some of those costs can be capitalized and depreciated or amortized. Depreciation and amortization is excluded from EBITDA. Which means those "expenses" vanish from EBITDA and your buyers have a higher metric to multiply.

- **Leases vs. Purchases**

Leasing cars and equipment keeps taxable income low, but it punishes EBITDA. Buy and capitalize them instead, and depreciation never hits EBITDA. Same assets, different story.

- **Normalizing One-Timers**

Pandemic subsidies, lawsuits, fires—one-time events get stripped out. You've heard me talk about add-backs.

- **Contract Alignment**

Construction firms, IT service shops, marketing agencies—SMBs often botch the accounting for long-term contracts. They book revenue when cash arrives or when invoices go out, not when work is earned. GAAP fixes that with percentage-of-completion. Sophisticated buyers correct the accounting which finds revenue to move forward, and suddenly EBITDA jumps.

• **Related-Party Cleanups**
Rent to your cousin's LLC. Payroll for your spouse. Messy personal perks. Sophisticated buyers strip it all out, normalizes it, and voilà—higher EBITDA.

SMBS WILL NEVER KNOW THE MILLIONS MISSED

You weren't trained to play this game, and neither was your bookkeeper. Most SMB CPAs are tax focused. Their job is to minimize taxes, not maximize valuation. And for years, that works fine—until the day you want to sell. Then it costs you millions.

Savvy strategic buyers don't see GAAP as a nuisance. They see it as a scalpel. They cut, carve, and recast until your numbers tell the most valuable story possible.

I had a client preparing to sell to private equity. Like most small businesses, they handled long-term contracts the "simple" way: revenue showed up when the invoice went out. But that's not how PE sees the world. Big firms and their QofE teams want revenue booked when it's earned.

The QofE firm came back with a $300K EBITDA reduction—from over-counting revenue. At a 7× multiple, that's $2.1 million off the table. I told my client, "I don't buy it. Let's rebuild revenue from the ground up. No stone unturned. I'm confident we'll recover that $300K—and maybe even more."

But after months of brutal negotiations, fatigue set in. My client was worn out. We collaborated and he told PE they had two choices: either give him the number he wanted or wait two weeks while we scrubbed every con-tract. PE agreed to his number, and we stopped digging.

Later, we figured out that the PE buyer was not giv-ing us credit for the revenue we had earned prior to close. Fortunately, just before close we clawed back much of the value. But it was a lot of stress and sleepless nights for my client. My client admitted later that he would never have known—he would have signed the deal and walked away, missing millions without realizing it.

Exhaustion makes you settle. Lack of preparation makes you blind. And in this case, both almost cost $2.1M. The truth is this simple: if the company had been accounting under GAAP for its long-term contracts before going to market, the scare would have been avoided. Proper prepa-ration locks in value. Fatigue and shortcuts cost you millions. Because in M&A, you don't know what you don't know—until it is too late.

> GAAP ISN'T WALL STREET'S PRIVATE PROPERTY, IT'S AVAILABLE TO ANYONE WILLING TO PAY BY THE RULES.

CONFETTI FOR MAIN STREET

Here's the best-kept secret: If PE and strategic buyers can do it, so can you. GAAP isn't Wall Street's private prop-erty, it's available to anyone willing to play by the rules.

I recently had a discovery meeting with two owners: one ran an online education company, and the other was building an AI product. Both were expensing major invest-ments that could have been capitalized. Within minutes, we reframed those costs under GAAP. Nothing in their business changed. But their EBITDA jumped by millions and so did their valuation. Proper accounting wins again!

That's the confetti moment. The realization that the missing millions weren't in some vault guarded by Wall Street. They were sitting in your own P&L, waiting to be dusted off and polished, and uncovered.

BUYER AND SELLER POV

Sellers: let's get you GAAP-smart before you go to market. Capitalize what lasts. Normalize expenses. Clean up related-party noise. Every step makes you command more millions.

And all buyers can look for sellers who haven't used the accounting wand. Poor accounting, tax-based books are your gold mine. That's instant upside you can harvest the day after close.

THE BOTTOM LINE

Private equity and strategic buyers do not wave magic wands, and they certainly aren't turning tricks, but I'm glad it caught your attention. Instead, they wave GAAP and the moment you understand that accounting is not just compliance but strategy, you'll never look at your financials the same way again.

If they can walk away worth millions more the day after close, why shouldn't you?

CHAPTER 8

DEAL STRUCTURE: ASSET OR EQUITY?

AND DEBUNKING "OMG, I'LL PAY TOO MUCH IN TAXES!"

The phone rang. The buyer answered.

The seller's voice was firm, almost smug:

"It has to be a stock deal to save on taxes—or no deal."

The buyer breathed deeply. He wanted the business so badly.

"Fine. Stock deal."

That night, he swirled the ice in his glass, top-shelf whiskey now tasting thin and bitter. He convinced himself it was smart—after all, the seller *insisted*. However, three months later, reality struck. An EPA violation from five years back. He was hit with cleanup costs that dwarfed any tax savings. Add in five-figure legal fees for dusty contract disputes he never signed, and suddenly, the whiskey went down like vinegar.

Panicked, he called his attorney.

"What about indemnifications in the purchase agreement? I thought I was protected."

The lawyer paused. Then sighed.

"On paper, yes. In practice? You may be holding the bag. The seller's indemnity is only as good as their willingness— and their bank account. And since he moved to Portugal two weeks after close…" The silence said everything.

That was the moment it landed. In a stock deal, you do not just buy the business. You buy its entire past. Every lawsuit. Every environmental mess. Every skeleton with teeth still sharp.

All because no one stopped to ask: *Was a stock deal really the answer?*

DEAL STRUCTURE MATTERS

The ice in that whiskey glass was not just melting; it was dissolving the illusion that deal structure is about taxes alone. The truth is: most sellers only know one drumbeat: minimize my taxes. Most CPAs echo it, louder. And buyers, eager to close, sometimes agree without realizing they have just inherited every ghost in the seller's closet. EPA violations, lawsuits, employee claims, warranty obligations—they don't vanish when the ink dries.

Deal structure is not just a tax exercise. It is the blueprint for who owns the risk, who holds the bag, and who sleeps at night after closing. Sellers hear "stock deal" and think less taxes. Buyers hear "asset deal" and think protection. Somewhere in the middle, both sides forget to ask the most important question: what are the real economics of signing this way or that way?

Let's not walk straight into regret, because you thought "stock vs. asset" was just to help the seller with taxes and the seller indemnifications in the agreement will make the buyer's risk and worries go away.

THE DEFAULT DEBATE: ASSET VS. STOCK

A potential battleground is asset deal versus stock deal. Sellers lean hard toward stock deals because they think it guarantees long-term capital gains at a 20% rate, versus the ordinary income rate of 35% (or higher, depending on their bracket and state). To them, that 15-point swing feels like a haircut on the purchase price.

Meanwhile, buyers often nod along, sometimes because they assume indemnifications will cover the risk, sometimes because they do not fully grasp what they are inheriting.

This is the technical truth:

- **Asset Deal** = buyer control. You pick the assets you want, leave behind the ones you do not, and get a step-up in basis for depreciation (which is a fancy way to say the buyer gets to take depreciation thus reducing taxes). You also leave most liabilities behind.

> DEAL STRUCTURE IS NOT JUST A TAX EXERCISE. IT IS THE BLUEPRINT FOR WHO OWNS THE RISK, WHO HOLDS THE BAG, AND WHO SLEEPS AT NIGHT AFTER CLOSING.

- **Stock Deal** = buyer inherits it all. Every contract, every skeleton in the closet, every risk hiding under the floorboards. Indemnifications in the purchase agreement may soften the blow, but they do not erase the risk.

Holli's way of saying it—an asset deal buys the horse. A stock deal buys the whole barn termites and all.

Even when sellers do get their "stock deal," it is not always the tax utopia they imagine. Portions of the purchase price tied to non-competes or consulting agreements still hit ordinary income. That part is negotiable, and often misunderstood, but it is very real.

There are moments when a stock deal makes strategic sense. But the decision cannot be driven by fear, noise from a CPA, or the reflex to minimize taxes at any cost.

INSIDE THE DEAL: WHAT REALLY HAPPENED

One of my clients, an entrepreneur, was about to make his very first acquisition in a buy-and-build strategy so he hired a well-known boutique M&A firm. They had all the polish: the credentials, the clean QofE process, and the fancy pitch deck. They presented themselves as the experts and I bought right in! But when the seller dug in and demanded a stock deal "for tax reasons," the buyer ran it by his fancy broker and then forwarded me the guidance he received. It was two sentences long:

"The valuation looks strong, so having it be an equity deal should be okay. Two items to keep in mind: You will not receive the benefit of a tax basis step-up, and you will assume historical liabilities."

That was it. No context. No explanation. No conversation about how this could alter the entire risk profile of his very first deal. And . . . does any CEO actually understand the ramifications of a *tax basis step-up*? That's just high-level accounting jargon. I was mad. For a first-time buyer, that kind of thin advice is not only unhelpful—it is dangerous. It leaves the client without a yardstick with which to measure risk, and worse, it normalizes the idea that a "stock deal equals fine" simply because the seller's CPA muttered the word "taxes." Let's be clear: the brokers get paid when the deal closes and the CPA's whole goal is to reduce taxes. Their incentives are not always aligned with protecting the buyer—or even the seller, for that matter. That's the conflict baked into the system. Someone has to be watching out for the true risks on both sides, and in this case, the advice was wholly inadequate.

That is when I stepped in. Here is what I told my client: "Proceed with caution. Sellers often push stock deals because they assume it is the only way to lock in capital gains treatment. But in businesses with few tangible assets—like this one—most of the gain would be taxed as capital gain even in an asset deal.

The seller is really saying: *I want to pay less in taxes.* That can be solved—without you inheriting a landfill of hidden liabilities. The worst mistake you can make is agreeing to the most buyer-hostile deal structure because someone waved the tax flag."

Post-script: I never received a response from the fancy firm and my client ended up not buying the business.

LET'S TALK TAXES (WITHOUT BEING YOUR CPA)

Full disclaimer: I'm not your tax advisor, I do not impersonate a tax professional on TV, and I don't even *like* talking about taxes. But I've sat in enough deal rooms to know this—smart people (including CPAs) oversimplify deal taxes in ways that create real risk. So, let's keep it simple, practical, and useful *without* creating risk.

Sellers default to "make it a stock sale" because they want long-term capital gains. When the seller's CPA says a stock deal is the *only* option, remember: the CPA's job is to minimize the seller's tax bill—not to protect their risk. Treat it as input, not a mandate. Get your own advisor and explore alternatives. This is negotiation, not gospel.

The big myth: "Asset sales automatically mean more taxes." Not always—especially in businesses that aren't asset-heavy. In many service companies, the bulk of the purchase price ends up in goodwill, which is taxed at capital gains rates anyway.

ASSET SALE–WHAT GETS TAXED HOW
(QUICK CHEAT SHEET)

Asset class	Typical examples	Seller tax treatment
Inventory	Raw materials, finished goods	Ordinary income
A/R & WIP	Unpaid invoices, work performed	Ordinary income
Furniture & equipment	Computers, machinery	Depreciation recapture (ordinary)
Goodwill / intangibles	Brand, customer list, reputation	Capital gains
Non-compete / consulting	Transition work, covenant not to compete	Ordinary income (allocations are negotiable)

Translation: If the target has minimal inventory, A/R, and WIP (hello, services), then, most of the price is good-will—already capital gains. The "ordinary income" slice is usually the smaller piece.

Now, I'd rather go to the dentist than get into depreciation recapture—but if we must, we must, so here goes. Depreciation recapture happens when the IRS says: "Hey seller: remember, how you wrote off those assets over the years? Well, we want some of that back as ordinary income." In an asset deal, if the buyer pays more than book value for your equipment, part of that gain is taxed at ordinary rates. But this isn't set in stone—the allocation schedule in the purchase agreement is where you negotiate how much ends up in recapture versus capital gains. Now the reality check for the buyer: even if an asset deal nudges a little more into ordinary income (think ~15 points vs. capital gains, subject to bracket and state), that delta is often *less than* what a stock deal costs you in extra diligence, legal, and risk transfer. QofE alone can double in scope and price for a stock deal because you're buying the whole history, not just the assets. Buyers can spend $60k–$100k to avoid a $20k tax difference. That math does not show you any love.

STOCK SALE–WHAT REALLY HAPPENS

Component	Description	Seller tax treatment
Purchase price for stock	Buyer purchases company equity	Typically, capital gains
Non–compete / consulting	Seller paid for transition or restraint	Ordinary income (and negotiable)

Most sellers *believe* a stock sale makes all proceeds long–term capital gains. Often true—but not all of it. Non–competes and consulting payments are still ordinary income, and the allocations are negotiable.

Holli's Heads–Up: In some cases, you can sign a stock deal and elect to treat it like an asset sale for tax purposes (see Section 338(h)(10) or 336(e)). That can give buyers a step–up in basis without changing the legal form. These elections aren't common. They require both sides to agree and the tax impact differs for each party. This is where a *good* tax advisor earns their keep. Ask: "Would a tax election help us meet in the middle?" (Please—do not ask me to explain the code sections at a dinner party. This is above my pay grade and ruins dessert.)

As we have discussed, buying a business in a stock deal is not just buying the company—it's buying every skeleton in the closet, whether you know what's there or not. It's like marrying someone and inheriting all their exes, unpaid parking tickets, and that time they "forgot" to file taxes in 2017. You do not just get the assets—you get all of the baggage.

> BUYING A BUSINESS IN A STOCK DEAL MEANS BUYING EVERY SKELETON IN THE CLOSET, WHETHER YOU KNOW WHAT'S THERE OR NOT.

RESPECT THE RISK

I spent part of my career in a 100% employee-owned company where risk was enemy number one. I had an amazing in-house attorney, and his entire job was to keep us from tripping on landmines. If a project manager wanted to tweak a contract, or if we signed a new vendor agreement, he would review it. Every time. It wasn't sexy. But it saved us from lawsuits, liability, and insurance hikes. Our professional liability premiums stayed low, and our legal fees were nearly nonexistent. Why? Because we *respected risk.*

Most SMB CEOs don't get that luxury. They juggle sales, payroll, vendors, and customers—you get used to the risk as "part of the job." And honestly, in the SMB trenches, sometimes it is. But here's where M&A is different: the stakes are higher. In a stock deal, risk follows you home. Every undisclosed liability, every lawsuit brewing under the surface, every sloppy contract suddenly has your name on it.

WHEN A STOCK SALE ACTUALLY MAKES SENSE

There are times when a stock deal makes the most sense. For example, industries where licenses or contracts don't transfer easily: medical clinics, labs, pharmacies, financial services firms, government contractors. In those cases, an asset deal means reapplying for approvals that can take months—or even years. A stock deal lets you keep the lights on, the licenses intact, and operations running smoothly.

Sometimes stock deals are chosen simply for ease of integration. I've seen this trend in private equity: they are sophisticated buyers who know how to weigh the risks. One of my clients sold to private equity, and at the LOI stage, the buyer reserved the right to structure the deal as either stock or asset. Their preference was stock—but they made it clear they'd walk away from that structure if diligence uncovered high risk. And diligence was deep: triple the time and extremely thorough. For them, paying up front and assuming risk was a calculated, professional choice.

For new buyers though, negotiating an asset deal is usually the safer route whenever possible. Unless there's a compelling reason, "tax savings" alone is rarely strong enough to justify that leap.

THE REAL COST OF A STOCK DEAL

When you buy stock, here's what you actually inherit: every historical liability, (including the ones you'll never find in diligence) litigation from old contracts, HR disputes, sloppy employee agreements, outdated handbooks, workers classified the wrong way, insurance gaps, unfiled taxes, missing licenses, weird state issues—and don't get me started on vendor, lease, and customer contracts that auto-renew. It's a diligence marathon. What might run you $30K in QofE for an asset deal can balloon to $60K, $90K or more in a stock deal. And even then, you're still exposed. No amount of diligence can fully scrub the skeletons hiding in a company's closet. You're paying more for the privilege of inheriting risks you can't even see yet. If you do go forward, budget for reps and warranties insurance. It's pricey, and it won't make the risk disappear, but it's at least a seatbelt in a car that's already missing airbags.

SOMETIMES IT'S CHEAPER TO SOLVE THE TAX PROBLEM

Because I worked for a company where all risk was to be mitigated, I successfully turned every potential stock deal into an asset deal. When I needed to, I paid the tax difference and sometimes I split it with the owner. I was buying service businesses at the time so ordinary income was minor.

Let's look at an example of how that may play out, say the total purchase price is $1M and it is allocated as such:

- $100K in A/R
- $50K in inventory
- $850K in goodwill

If the ordinary income tax rate is ~35% and capital gains is ~20%, that 15% difference on $150K in A/R and inventory means the seller pays ~$22,500 more in taxes in an asset deal.

You, the buyer, might easily spend more than that on <u>extra diligence and legal fees</u> (in the above case you will) for a stock deal—and still carry more risk.

In many cases, it is cleaner and cheaper to:

- Offer a price adjustment and increase the purchase price slightly to cover the seller's added tax.
- Reallocate portions of the deal strategically with the seller's tax advisor.

All while preserving the asset structure and protecting yourself from inherited messes.

DEAL STRUCTURE SNAPSHOT

Category	Asset Sale	Stock Sale
Tax Basis Step-Up*	Yes	No
Historical Liabilities	Not inherited (typically)	Inherited
License Transfers	Re-apply required	Retained
Buyer Risk	Lower (with diligence)	Higher
Legal & Accounting Costs	Moderate	High
Regulatory Friction	Higher	Lower (in some industries)

*Tax Basis Step-Up—which is a fancy way to say the buyer gets to take depreciation thus reducing taxes. This means the assets the buyer purchases are recorded at fair-market value then depreciated for tax purposes. For example, a truck's fair-market value may be $50k but the seller has already depreciated it to $10k on their books. The buyer gets to record the asset at $50k and then use the depreciation for tax.

BOTTOM LINE

As a CFO, I hated stock deals because I did not like expensive surprises. And stock deals, are surprise factories. So, when a seller says, "I want a stock deal to reduce my taxes," Your educated response should be: "Let's talk about the actual numbers—and the actual risk." You can often solve the seller's tax concern without putting yourself in legal jeopardy. But if a stock deal is truly necessary—because of licensing, continuity, or deal dynamics—then do it with eyes wide open. Bring your A-team. Budget for real diligence. And protect yourself with reps, warranties, and tail insurance (more on that in chapter 13). That team should include a qualified M&A attorney—especially when navigating deal structure, indemnities, and contract exposure. I don't want your millions disappear because you walked into a deal structure without making a fully informed decision.

CHAPTER 9

BUYING–*WITHOUT* BUYING THE FARM

WHY BUYERS AND SELLERS SHOULD CONSIDER CREATIVE CARVE OUTS.

"I only wanted her Team."

The buyer had been eyeing this boutique firm for years. The founder had a sharp little brand—tight delivery, loyal clients, a team that looked like they actually liked working together. But the financials? Even after generous normalization, the EBITDA refused to play nice. The full acquisition price made zero sense.

Still, her gut kept nudging, "There's value here. I don't need the whole company—I need her people. I need those clients." So, she re-wrote the playbook:

- Hire the top performers directly, with signing bonuses.
- Take over three key customer contracts.
- Pay the seller a one-time transition fee for goodwill and warm handoffs.
- Draft a non-solicit. Walk away clean.

No entity transfer. No liability assumption. No messy back-office entanglements. The deal closed in 45 days. Six months later, the buyer had everything she wanted—and none of the integration chaos. The seller had what she wanted too: her company sold, her people protected, and her legacy intact. The buyer didn't buy the company; she bought the outcome.

A SLICE OF THE WHOLE PIE

Most people think "acquisition" means buying the whole thing. But seasoned buyers (and smart sellers) know there's another way. Sometimes the best play is to take just the piece that matters most, this is known as a carve-out.

A carve-out happens when a company sells or separates just one part of its business—like a product line or division. The parent company keeps its core, while the carved-out piece becomes its own standalone business, often under new ownership.

> SOMETIMES THE BEST PLAY IS TO TAKE JUST THE PIECE THAT MATTERS MOST, THIS IS KNOWN AS A CARVE-OUT.

Companies usually do this to sharpen their focus, raise capital, meet regulatory requirements, or unlock value that might be hidden inside a larger structure. In other words, a carve-out is about streamlining the parent company and giving the unit that was "carved out" a better shot at growth on its own under the new buyer.

These deals are faster. Cleaner. Sharper. They don't always make headlines, but they quietly create massive wins. For buyers, carve-outs cut the fat and let you buy the meat. For sellers, they create an exit option when the full company price tag isn't realistic, or when keeping a portion makes more sense than selling everything.

Instead of taking on all the liabilities, overhead, and legacy headaches, the buyer can focus on the assets that actually move the needle. That could mean:

- **The people**—a team or leadership group ("group hire" or acquihire)
- **The clients**—a set of contracts or relationships that keep the revenue flowing
- **The book**—a defined portfolio of business or a specific product/service line
- **The footprint**—regional rights, a territory carve-out, or expansion of a platform play
- **The brand/IP**—trademarks, technology, or creative assets you can leverage

Think of it as buying outcomes. You get the talent, the customers, or the rights you need without absorbing the seller's back-office mess, debts, or cultural landmines.

THE CREATIVE CARVE-OUT TOOLKIT

Type	What You're Acquiring	Why It Works
Group Hire	Key team or leaders	Secures talent + momentum, avoids liabilities
Client Roll-In	Book of business or client contracts	Instant revenue, minimal integration hassle
Territory Carve-Out	Rights to regions or offerings	Perfect for franchise or platform expansion

Type	What You're Acquiring	Why It Works
IP/Brand Licensing	Tech, trademarks, content	Use proven brand equity without full acquisition
Partial Buyout	Minority stake or single unit	Participate in growth with limited control shift

None of these ideas are new. But few people execute them well because they assume "buying the business" is the only option on the table. The reality? These carve-outs can be far more strategic than a traditional purchase.

WHEN TO USE THIS STRUCTURE

Creative carve-outs aren't for every situation. But they shine when the full deal just doesn't make sense, or doesn't need to. Buyers, reach for this structure when:

1. The financials don't support a full acquisition, but the team or client roster is too good to pass up.
2. A seller wants a partial exit, or a phased transition instead of walking away cold.
3. You're expanding into a new market and want plug-and-play growth, not a year of integration headaches.
4. You're after the outcome—not the risk.

Think of it as deal minimalism: strip away the extra and keep only what matters.

Sellers, you reach this structure when:

1. You want partial liquidity without full exit.
2. A division no longer fits your strategy but has value to others.
3. You want to preserve legacy for staff or clients while still getting paid for what you've built.

DIAGRAM: TRADITIONAL VS. CREATIVE CARVE-OUT

Here's the contrast:

	Traditional Acquisition	Creative Carve-Out
Legal Entity	Stock deal: Entity Acquired Asset deal: Entity not Acquired	No entity transferred
Liabilities	Assumed or negotiated	Generally excluded
Structure	*APA or SPA + Reps/ Warranties	Offer Letters, Assignments, Non-Solicits
Speed	3 to 12 months	30–45 days
Integration	Full integration required	Limited or none

*APA is Asset Purchase Agreement and SPA or EPA is Stock or Equity Purchase Agreement—complex agreements prepared by expensive M&A attorneys.

The beauty of a carve-out is speed and simplicity. But don't confuse simple with sloppy.

STRUCTURING THESE DEALS

These deals still need sharp legal framing, they aren't handshake agreements over lunch. This is where your M&A attorney earns their fee because each one requires a different legal lense.

- **Employee Transfers** → Offer letters, IP assignments, non-solicits, and sometimes non-competes (check your state laws).
- **Client Contracts** → Watch for anti-assignment or change-of-control clauses. Get them reviewed before you bank on the revenue.
- **IP & Brand Rights** → Verify who actually owns it. If IP sits in a founder's name or with a contractor, you'll need assignments.
- **Territory Carve-Outs** → Define the map clearly. Exclusivity and non-competes matter.

A NOTE ON PRICING & VALUATION

Unlike full acquisitions with established multiples, these partial deals are harder to price. There's no "Kelley Blue Book" for carve-outs. You can't Google "what multiple do I pay for a team hire?" and get a reliable answer. This is not a back-of-the-napkin guess. It's math plus judgment. Valuation here depends on:

- Revenue quality and stickiness—*Will those clients stay after the handoff?*
- Cost structure—*What expenses come with the carve-out, what stays behind?*

- Cash flow modeling—*What is actually added to your bottom line, risk-adjusted?*

If you're not sure, bring in an M&A advisor who's priced carve-outs before. (Like me—I mean truly, you should bring one in anyway.)

SELLER POV: WHY YOU MIGHT SAY "YES" OR INITIATE THIS YOURSELF

Carve-outs aren't just clever plays for savvy buyers—they're also powerful strategies for smart sellers. Not every founder is ready (or able) to hand over the keys to the whole kingdom. But that doesn't mean there isn't value locked inside that can be released. Sometimes the smartest move is trimming one piece that creates liquidity, secures continuity for employees or clients, or frees the founder to focus on what's next.

> THE BEAUTY OF A CARVE-OUT IS SPEED AND SIMPLICITY. BUT DON'T CONFUSE SIMPLE WITH SLOPPY.

Sometimes it makes sense to trim a piece that no longer excites you or fits with your vision. Maybe it's a business line that's stable but stagnant, one you'd rather see in someone else's hands while you focus on growth. Or maybe it's your team—you know they'd thrive with the backing of a bigger platform, and a carve-out gives them that runway.

You might also decide to sell a book of business you've spent years building but you are ready to focus on something else. You can monetize what you've created without surrendering your entire company. And for many sellers, there's the personal factor: carving out parts of the company can preserve continuity for the clients and employees you care about most, while still creating liquidity for you.

That's the flexibility of carve-outs. They let you get paid for value you've already built, without walking away from everything you've poured into the business. It's not an all-or-nothing exit—it's a way to shape your own terms and timeline.

WHEN THE RIGHT PLAY DOESN'T CLOSE

A client of mine spotted a firm with everything he wanted: a coveted client list, a creative team, and market presence. But the business had a bloated back office and no real profitability. Buying the entire company made no sense.

His strategy was smart: he would offer jobs to the top three employees and purchase the top ten client contracts. He would leave the rest behind—overhead, debt, and inefficiency. On paper, it was clean and fast. The seller, however, wasn't ready to move forward that way, and that's why it's important to acknowledge that not every creative carve-out closes.

But the strategy itself works. I've used it myself. As a buyer in the engineering space, I structured small acquisitions this way—picking up sellers, their staff, and their backlog without taking on the full company. It gave me the value I wanted (talent and pipeline) without the drag of legacy systems and liabilities.

Sometimes these deals land. Sometimes they don't. But the lesson is this: carve-outs are a legitimate play. Even if one doesn't close, the approach itself is a powerful way to think about value beyond the full-entity acquisition.

BUYERS: DO NOT SKIP DILIGENCE

Even when you are not acquiring the entire company, diligence is not optional—it is your seatbelt. A creative carve-out or partial acquisition can feel deceptively simple, but the risks are still real, and they hide in the details.

Start with the people. Who are you actually getting? Are they the reason the business works, and will they stay after the deal? A team that looks great on paper can unravel quickly if retention, culture fit, or incentives are off.

Next, look at the contracts. Are they assignable? Do they allow for a clean hand-off, or will you be left renegotiating with customers who suddenly feel *they* have all the leverage?

Intellectual property and brand rights can be another trap. Make sure the seller truly owns what they are handing over. If code was written by contractors or branding lives in a cousin's LLC, you may not own the asset you thought you bought.

And do not forget the customers. Are they satisfied? Are they loyal to the company or to the founder who is leaving? Retention and stickiness matter more than glossy revenue charts.

Finally, get clear on the boundaries: what exactly is included, and what is left behind? Carve-outs are about precision. A single overlooked exclusion can leave you without a key system, piece of IP, or license you assumed was in the package.

Skipping these steps is how "simple" deals turn into costly, complicated headaches. Light diligence is still diligence—and it is the only way to make sure you are buying the outcome you think you are.

THE BOTTOM LINE:
BUY THE OUTCOME, NOT THE OVERHEAD

Creative carve-outs are power moves. They let you buy the exact result you want—talent, clients, IP, or market presence—without inheriting the back-office mess, legacy liabilities, or bloated systems. These deals still need precision. Get your lawyer involved early. Nail down assignments, contracts, and protections. When structured right, carve-outs are quiet revolutions fast, clean, strategic.

> SOMETIMES THE BEST DEALS ARE NOT THE ONES YOU FIND LISTED— THEY ARE THE ONES YOU ENGINEER. AND OFTENTIMES, THESE ARE THE DEALS THAT CHANGE EVERYTHING.

Sometimes the best deals are not the ones you find listed—they are the ones you engineer. And oftentimes, these are the deals that change everything.

CHAPTER 10

THE DANCE NOBODY WANTS TO LEARN–BUT MUST!

STEPPING CAREFULLY THROUGH WORKING CAPITAL

The conference room was quiet. The buyer sat gleefully, relishing his win of the day in a blissful moment of solace. The lights in the hallway had already flickered off. The deal was inked only moments ago. Everyone smiled. Everyone shook hands and left—including the cash.

The buyer sat alone in the afterglow, when the controller pushed open the conference door with a one-knuckle knock, "Sorry to disturb you sir, but how are we paying the new team on Friday?"

The buyer leaned forward with a quizzical look. He hadn't thought of that. The deal included no cash. No A/R. Just a company shell. The seller was gone and payroll was two days away. He called the seller. "So, can we keep the accounts receivable?" The seller retorted, "You bought the business."

That was the moment the buyer realized: the awkward "dance" over working capital never played out. They discussed everything else. They were all in the ballroom but never waltzed out onto the floor. Now, he was left alone to face the music.

THE AWKWARD DANCE

Working capital. It isn't glamorous and it is very much an awkward dance that few understand. However, if you don't do the dance, or if you miss the timing, you could literally miss out on millions. If you want a clean deal, you have to learn the awkward dance of negotiating working capital—and stay in time with the music!

Working Capital is not the earnout cliffhanger or the headline valuation. It is the quiet number that makes or breaks cash flow from day one. Negotiating working capital can mean putting your deal on life support. Most sellers, and plenty of buyers, don't really understand how it works. Everyone nods at the LOI when it calls for "three months of working capital." But when the agreement stage arrives, sellers often assume they can take everything with them and buyers assume it's all staying. Sellers assume, "I sold the business, I get the cash and the receivables." And buyers assume, "I bought the business, I get the receivables." Both are wrong—unless the "choreography" is clearly defined in advance. I have a three-part framework I'm going to walk you through, but first, I need a one-on-one privately with the sellers and then the buyers. Hold please.

HOLLI'S HANG OUT WITH THE SELLERS

Sellers, I know what you're thinking: *Those receivables are mine. I worked for them. I created them while I still owned the business. They are mine to take.*

That feels logical—and in some very small transactions, that's the way it's handled. But in most deals, especially with savvy buyers, whether it's a PE firm, a strategic, or even an SBA buyer with good advisors, receivables are part of the working capital handoff. Why? Because the buyer is paying for a business that can actually run the day after closing.

If you sweep up all the receivables and walk out the door, the buyer has to inject more money into the business just to make payroll and pay vendors after the close. That means they effectively paid a premium for your company—and goodwill evaporates fast.

This is my suggestion to help you avoid getting pinned into a deal at the last minute: set the purchase price you're happy with, and factor in delivering a normalized level of working capital. If there's more than the target, it flows back to you in the true-up. You're not giving anything away—you're getting paid for it.

Without stepping into this "working capital waltz" you risk losing an otherwise solid deal in the final stretch. Go on the offensive. Address it early, and you protect both your payday and your legacy. Now, let me have a word with the buyers . . .

HOLLI'S HANG OUT WITH THE BUYERS

Buyers: do not assume you're automatically getting working capital. Smaller sellers (and sometimes their brokers) may insist they take it all with them.

If you don't surface the issue early, you risk hitting the finish line only to discover you need a bigger loan just to make payroll. That means you've paid a premium for a business that can't fund itself. Many SBA lenders know this—which is why they quietly add working capital into loans.

Build it into your financing and your enterprise value and don't tiptoe around it. Start the waltz and set up the framework right from the start.

BREAKING DOWN WORKING CAPITAL

We've touched on this a bit so far, but truly, working capital is the lifeblood of any business. In practical terms, it is simply the short-term fuel—receivables, inventory, prepaid expenses minus bills you owe that you haven't paid yet. That's it. Simple math, that yields messy debates.

In M&A, deals are usually debt-free and cash-free. The seller takes the cash at close and pays off debt and transaction expenses. The seller typically delivers some level of working capital i.e. enough receivables, inventory, and other short-term assets to cover payroll, vendors, and operations the very next morning.

That's why this quiet little number kills deals. It cannot be ignored, or millions will go missing . . . and fast!

LET'S GO TO DANCE CLASS

If you've ever taken a dance class, you know things get easier when you break them down step by step so here is my 3-Part Framework for the Working Capital Waltz. (No tu-tu required.) Buyers, you are leading on this one . . .

Step 1 - LOI / Discovery: First, you need to assess where everyone stands. At the LOI stage, you almost never have enough detail to establish a target number. That's fine. Your job at this point is to flesh out positions and lock down intent.

- **Goal:** Do both sides agree that *some* working capital stays with the business so it can run post-closing?

- **Who may resist:** smaller sellers, some brokers, and even a few CPAs. Treat this as a temperature check and a teaching moment.
- **What to write in the LOI:** *Seller will deliver a normalized level of Net Working Capital at closing, calculated as current assets (excluding cash and cash equivalents) minus current liabilities (excluding debt and debt-like items), consistent with historical accounting practices, with a post-closing true-up if actual is above/below target.*
- **"Why not just write** *3 months of WC* **in the LOI?"** I hear people say this all the time and truly, it's lazy short-hand. It ignores seasonality, project timing, and nuances that set you up for surprises after close. Formulate intent now and save precision for diligence.

> WORKING CAPITAL IS THE QUIET NUMBER THAT MAKES OR BREAKS CASH FLOW FROM DAY ONE.

Principle: Working capital should be neutral enough for the buyer to operate the business as it was historically, with excess returned to the seller. No buyer windfalls, no seller haircuts.

Step 2 – Diligence / Education: Now it's time to replace guesses and assumption with actual numbers. In diligence, once you have data, you move from concept to math—and you keep educating as needed.

- **Perform Baseline Calculations:** Review monthly Net Working Capital and compute a 12-month average, or longer if needed.
- **Adjust for reality:**
  - Seasonality or project cycles → use seasonally adjusted averages.

o A/R quality → exclude very old/likely uncollectible balances.
o Inventory → write down obsolete/slow-moving.
o Include any accrued expenses that have been "forgotten."
o Stay consistent with historical accounting practices.

Here is a simple example:
A/R = $200K, Inventory = $0, Prepaids = $0, Credit card/ AP = $50K → Average WC = **$150K** *This would be the target, assuming operations were stable.*

Quick Gut-Check:
There is another way I like to check to make sure the historical working capital is sufficient. The calculation above implies and assumes that the company is historically operating with enough working capital, but the following calculation will tell you if that is true or not.

- $973k annual revenue = $2,666 daily revenue
- $200k A/R divided by $2,666 = 75 days to collect A/R
- $722k annual expenses = $1,979 daily expenses
- 75 days x $1,979 = $148k
  $148k is the working capital needed

Historical average ($150K) sits at the coverage floor (~$150K). If the average falls below the floor, expect a *cash squeeze.*

Holli's Take: Education doesn't stop here. If a seller calls working capital a "price haircut," it is an opportunity to reframe and say market multiples already assume working capital is included. If the buyer must borrow just to fund normal operations, then the business was purchased at a price above its market-supported value.

Step 3 - APA / Lock and True Up: Lock in the target number to protect both sides. When you move to the purchase agreement, make the working capital rules unmistakable.

- **Set the Target:** Insert the dollar target (from diligence) into a schedule to the APA.
- **Define the Math:** Consistent with historical practices; list inclusions/exclusions: no cash, no debt-like items, treatment of aged A/R, obsolete inventory, customer deposits, accrued payroll/bonuses, taxes payable, etc.
- **Cut-off & Timing:** State the balance sheet date/time for the closing calculation and a post-close true-up window (e.g., 60–90 days).
- **Closing Statement:** Outline who prepares it (buyer), when it's delivered, a seller review period, and method for dispute resolution.
- **Make it Neutral:** If actual WC > Target → increase price (or cash to seller). If actual WC < Target → decrease price (or pull from escrow). Neutral means the buyer gets what's needed to operate; no payment required to either the buyer or the seller.

HOLLI'S WORKING CAPITAL WALTZ REVIEW

Because repetition is the mother of mastery, here is a quick review of the steps to the "Working Capital Waltz." Remember, buyers lead, sellers follow and try not to step on anybody's toes!

Step 1 - LOI / Discovery:
Buyer sets intent in writing
Seller acknowledges concept
Broker/CPA looped in early

Step 2 – Diligence / Education:
Buyer's finance team (or QofE) runs the math
Seller provides monthly detail
Both sides adjust for seasonality/quality.

Step 3 – APA / Lock & True-Up:
Lawyers codify definitions and mechanics.
After closing the Buyer prepares post-close statement
Neutral true-up settles the difference.

> COLLECTIONS DON'T
> REFILL THE TANK;
> THEY JUST PLUG THE
> HOLE THAT'S ALREADY
> BEEN DUG.

Neutrality is the guiding principle: enough WC stays so the buyer can operate, and any excess above the target flows back to the seller. No windfalls. No haircuts. No working capital pickpocketing on either side.

THE 90-DAY STANDOFF

In one deal I worked on, the buyer and seller locked horns over the working capital target. The buyer wanted 90 days of working capital—about $700,000. The seller insisted 60 days, or $500,000, was plenty.

We compromised: the buyer would get the full $700,000 at closing, and after 90 days, if they didn't need the extra $200,000, the surplus would be refunded to the seller. Fair enough. But then the seller's attorney came back with a twist: the buyer could only "keep" $500,000. Any collections above that amount during the first 90 days would go straight back to the seller—whether or not the business still needed the cash.

Now picture the buyer's reality. Day 30: working capital dips to $400,000. Payroll is due. Vendors are waiting.

The buyer scrambles—dipping into personal funds or borrowing to cover the gap. By Day 90, collections finally climb to $550,000. But under the seller's formula, anything over $500,000 is swept back to the seller. The buyer is still stuck repaying the loan they took just to cover payroll.

Now, look me straight in the eyes while I tell you this: When it comes to working capital, if you start behind, you don't "catch up." Collections don't refill the tank; they just plug the hole that's already been dug. Unless the business grows, the shortfall follows you month after month. And when sellers try to engineer clawbacks like this, it's a red flag. The deal isn't just about numbers anymore—it's about trust and education. If discovery and alignment weren't done early, you'll see it in convoluted formulas like this one.

A word of caution: when either party tries to overcomplicate the calculation, like in the example above, it's a red flag. It should not be further complicated—there's a problem underneath. That's what happens when discovery and education aren't done properly early.

THE $1M SURPRISE

In another deal, my client was selling to PE. Working capital was to be based on historical levels, per the LOI. We were two weeks from close. Still no WC calculation in the drafts. Finally, one shows up—fine, reasonable. Then, the night before close, the buyer says: "We're excluding unbilled A/R from the valuation." We were talking about $1M of revenue earned, but not yet billed on long-term projects and they weren't going to give credit for it. It was a dramatic scene and suddenly the deal looked shaky. We could bill for it, but the PE folks and their accountant told us we would be breaking reps and warranties if we billed the night before closing. I was determined to solve this dilemma. This was $1M of real cash to the seller. We called our attorney who confirmed it would not be a breach.

PE backed down and said we didn't have to bill it. They finally agreed to include unbilled A/R in the WC true-up. My client kept the $1M and the champagne was flowing the next day. My client told me later; he wouldn't have known that they were taking that money if I had not been there. He wasn't aware he could push back. And that's how millions go missing. It wasn't that PE was doing anything wrong per se, they were negotiating, but the unexperienced seller just "didn't know what he didn't know."

This is my lesson: Working capital is not a leverage tool. Don't let the buyer use it to claw back your deal. Make sure the definitions of what is considered working capital are properly outlined in the agreement. In this case, working capital was defined as historical, and PE argued that unbilled A/R hadn't been historically included in our own figures. That may have been true—but they were still trying to walk away with a $1M upswing. Lock that definition in!

TRUE-UP MATH AND HOLDBACKS

Almost all deals have a true-up—because no one knows the exact numbers on the day of closing. Within 60-90 days post-close, buyer and seller compare actual working capital at closing to the agreed target. If the actual is greater than the target, the seller is paid the difference by the buyer. If the actual is less than the target, the buyer is reimbursed by the seller. This protects both sides from timing issues.

A holdback (or escrow) is sometimes used as *one way* to make sure the true-up gets settled cleanly—but it's not universal.

- **With a holdback**: A slice of the purchase price is set aside at closing. If the true-up goes against the seller, funds are pulled from there. If not needed, the seller gets it back.
- **Without a holdback**: Buyer pays the full purchase price at close. If the true-up later favors the buyer, they have to collect from the seller directly—usually by invoice. This can be fine if there's trust and both sides are financially strong, but it introduces collection risk.

When Holdbacks Show Up:

- **More common** in PE, bank-financed, or larger deals (institutional buyers want certainty).
- **Less common** in smaller, relationship-driven or SBA deals.

THE BOTTOM LINE—WHERE
THE MISSING MILLIONS HIDE

Working capital is not applause-worthy, but it is deal-critical. Miss it, and millions slip away: buyers overpay, sellers feel cheated, and deals stall.

When handled correctly, working capital is neutral: there's enough for the buyer to operate historically and any excess is returned to the seller. It should never be a buyer's windfall—or a seller's haircut.

Buyers, lead the dance by surfacing it early, educating with data, and locking it down in the purchase agreement. Sellers, walk the floor knowing this isn't giving something away—it's delivering what you've already been paid for—and get paid for it!

Get it right, and both sides leave the ballroom standing tall. Get it wrong, and the music stops before the dance ever begins.

CHAPTER 11

DILIGENCE–JUDGEMENT DAY FOR DEALS

WHERE DEALS EITHER MARCH TO THE CLOSING TABLE . . . OR THE GRAVEYARD.

The deal was sooo close. The LOI was signed and just "like that" the buyer hired a CPA firm for the Quality of Earnings (QofE). The buyer winced at the $28,000 price tag but it was her first deal, and she was determined to do it right.

On paper, the seller boasted a glimmering $500,000 EBITDA. But the QofE had a cruel way of stripping off the glitter. When the report landed, EBITDA shrank to $300,000—a forty percent reduction.

Meanwhile, the lawyer hammered away at the asset purchase agreement. More billable hours. More momentum. The clock ticked louder with each draft. The buyer wrestled with herself. *How can this be renegotiated? Should this be renegotiated?* The seller was not flexible in the price and was not going to go for a bigger earnout. *Should she risk losing the deal she had spent months chasing?* She liked the seller. They had broken bread and built rapport. It felt personal. But numbers have no regard for friendship, or for shared appetizers.

The deal collapsed. Not with drama, not with shouting, just the quiet inevitability of a structure that could not hold. It ended where so many do—in diligence, the place where numbers tell the truth and deal falls apart.

TO DO DUE DILIGENCE OR NOT TO DO DUE DILIGENCE . . .

Buyers, no short-cuts here: you cannot skip diligence. Ever. It is the spotlight that reveals whether the seller's story holds up. Deals don't fall apart because of diligence itself—they fall apart because diligence uncovers what is already there that you can't see. If you want to protect your millions, you have to look under the hood, not just at the shiny paint job.

Diligence is not glamorous. (Are you catching on here? Not much about the process is.) It is slow, expensive, and uncomfortable. It tests every assumption made at the LOI stage. Numbers that once looked shiny and convincing are suddenly stripped bare, reconciled, prodded, and verified. A seller's story meets a buyer's microscope.

> DEALS DON'T FALL APART BECAUSE OF DILIGENCE ITSELF—THEY FALL APART BECAUSE DILIGENCE UNCOVERS WHAT IS ALREADY THERE THAT YOU CAN'T SEE.

For buyers, it is the moment where "gut feel" gives way to hard data. For sellers, it is the moment where preparation—or lack of it—shows up in black and white. And for both sides, it is the moment where emotions run highest: excitement, fear, urgency, fatigue.

There is no romance in diligence. But diligence itself is not a villain. It is the truth-teller. Done right, it protects both parties, sometimes by killing a deal before the damage gets far worse. It's like being in a new relationship that looks so promising—until you ask for the password on your beloved's phone. This is where you verify the story.

Let's just take a good hard look at what actually

happens here: the roles of QofE, the questions lawyers never stop asking, and the subtle negotiations that creep in once reality replaces projection. We will step into the mechanics of what is tested, what is uncovered, and why smart buyers and sellers embrace diligence as their ally, even when it hurts. Because in M&A, this is not the paperwork stage, it is diligence discipline. To be a master of acquisitions, diligence is for you.

WHAT IS DILIGENCE?

People toss around the word *diligence* like it is a box you check. It is not. Diligence is not just financial, and it is not just legal—it is the full teardown of a machine you are about to buy or sell. Every gear, every belt, every moving part is pulled apart to see whether it runs the way the story says it does. If you walk in unprepared, buyers will find the loose threads, and every one of them will cost you money.

Diligence sweeps across every corner of the business:

- **Financial**—Quality of earnings, tax exposure, cash flow truth.
- **Legal**—Contracts, ownership, liabilities that do not vanish with the seller.
- **HR**—Payroll practices, hidden liabilities, employee retention risks.
- **Operational**—Supply chain, systems, processes that make-or-break daily execution.
- **Technology**—Data security, licenses, whether the tech actually scales.
- **Insurance**—Coverage, claims history, gaps that leave you exposed.

- **Compliance**—Licenses, permits, regulatory requirements that can halt business cold.

THE HEART OF DILIGENCE IS FINANCIAL FIRST

Immediately after the LOI is financial diligence. This is the deal crucible. Go all in now, because if the numbers do not hold up, nothing else matters. Push through this stage, and your odds of closing rise dramatically.

Sellers: you will be required to set up a data room. *What's a data room?* In the old days, it was a literal room, usually at an attorney's office where binders of documents and data related to the transaction were safely kept. Today, we do this virtually. The integrity of the data room is critical. Think of it like a shared digital vault *you* control—where *you* upload every financial and legal document for the buyer to review. It's your responsibility to ensure everything in there is accurate, consistent, and tells the story you want the buyer to read. As the seller, you control what goes into it and everything uploaded should be verified. For example, if your balance sheet shows $1M in accounts receivable (AR), then your AR aging report had better be equal to $1M. Same with P&Ls: if you show a $5M revenue figure on one version and $4M on another, you might as well invite a price reduction before the buyer even arrives. Consistency and accuracy are where trust is developed, and risks are reduced.

In my world, more than half of deals fail in financial diligence. And they should. Buying a company takes money and commitment and this is where both get tested. This is where bad stories get exposed. Sellers, your job is to prepare your financial story so it can survive this scrutiny. Buyers, your job is not to build the seller's story.

Your job is to test it, verify it, and make sure it is real—QofE will do that for you. Sellers propose EBITDA. Buyers verify it.

WHAT IS A QofE?

The QofE is a specialized consulting agreement with a CPA firm (it is not an audit) that many buyers use to validate the seller's EBITDA. Who does it? CPA firms specializing in M&A transactions—not your everyday CPA.

What it does:

- Validates EBITDA and whether it is actually repeatable
- Reviews revenue trends, customer concentration, and seasonality
- Tests add-backs and normalization adjustments
- Highlights unusual swings in revenue and expenses
- Anything else the buyer would like to focus on financially

Nothing carries more weight in this phase than the QofE. It is a flashlight aimed squarely at the beating heart of the business: earnings. The QofE strips away owner perks, timing quirks, and wishful thinking.

QofE says, "This is what the business really earns." The seller's stories about "growth just around the corner" are measured against data. The buyer's confidence in the deal hangs on whether the numbers hold.

DO I *HAVE* TO DO A QofE?

Not always, but I will repeat that buyers cannot skip financial diligence; therefore, some level of diligence still must be done or there are significant risks. In smaller deals, a full QofE may not be required—especially if a buyer has internal financial expertise or brings in a trusted advisor. Sometimes, banks *may* require a QofE if you're financing part of the deal. Other times, they just want to see clean financials and solid projections.

What matters most is you must have someone independently test the numbers. Whether it is a QofE firm, a CPA, or a strategic advisor, someone with deal experience must vet the EBITDA and flag risks before you commit capital.

WHAT DOES A QofE COST?

Most first-time buyers are shocked by the cost. Twenty to thirty thousand dollars feels like an enormous check to write for a report. But sophisticated buyers know better. A QofE is an insurance policy against regret. Sellers: if your buyer is getting a QofE, they are serious.

Deal Size	Typical Cost Range
Small deals	$12K - $28K
Lower middle market	$20K - $50K
Middle market	$50K - $100K+

M&A dollars start adding up fast once diligence begins. Know your spend threshold early.

DELIVERABLES ARE EVOLVING

Years ago, QofEs were static binders of numbers and footnotes. Today, deliverables are sharp, visual, and tailored to decision-making. Buyers expect dashboards, red flags, and concise walkaways. They want to know not only whether EBITDA holds, but whether revenue trends are sustainable, whether customers are concentrated, whether margins are fragile.

The change in deliverables reflects a broader shift: diligence is no longer a formality. It is an active strategy. It does not just validate numbers; it shapes negotiation, informs financing, and influences whether a deal closes at all.

- The Old Way: Big glossy reports (some buyers still want these)
- The New Way: Data books, Excel models, dashboards

Your QofE output should give you financial clarity and risks identified, not just paperwork.

> DILIGENCE IS NOT JUST FINANCIAL, AND IT IS NOT JUST LEGAL—IT IS THE FULL TEARDOWN OF A MACHINE YOU ARE ABOUT TO BUY OR SELL.

IF QofE LOWERS EBITDA–DO I RETRADE THE DEAL?

Welcome to the *art* of M&A. Numbers will shift during diligence—that is a guarantee. The real question is how much movement is too much. Here is the yardstick I use (credit to Adam Coffey in *Empire Builder*):

If EBITDA shifts less than 10%, you keep marching forward. That is the normal noise of business. When the swing is between 10% and 30%, you stop and renegotiate—because those dollars matter and the deal you thought you were doing has changed. And if EBITDA shifts more than 30%? That is not a deal anymore. That is a different company. Close the book and walk away.

THE 47% REDUCTION DEAL

Another client I was working with was excited about her first purchase. This was the first step in her buy-and-build strategy, and she wanted to get it right. The LOI was signed, the lawyer was drafting the asset purchase agreement, and momentum was building.

Then diligence began.

On paper, the seller had presented a very healthy EBITDA. But when we rolled up our sleeves and looked at the trailing twelve months, the numbers told a different story. EBITDA was 47% less than what was offered at the LOI stage. Nearly half the value was gone.

The truth came out quickly. A key staff member had left and had taken clients with them. The revenue loss was already baked into the numbers. My client tried to salvage the deal, offering less cash at close, a larger and longer earnout—but the seller walked away.

The deal should have died the moment the numbers told their story. Instead, legal documents were already being drafted, legal fees were piling up, and the momentum of the deal was in full swing.

FINANCIAL DILIGENCE FIRST
(ESPECIALLY IN SMALL DEALS)

In the world of $1M–$10M acquisitions, you do not have unlimited dollars to throw around. Every professional you bring in—the M&A advisor, the attorney, the HR consultant, the compliance specialist—turns on their meter the second you say "go." If the deal collapses in financial diligence, you have just paid for work you did not need. That is why I always advise: clear financial diligence first.

Financial diligence is the gatekeeper. If EBITDA cannot hold, or if cash flow is weaker than advertised, nothing else matters. Why pay lawyers to review contracts on a deal that is already upside down?

GET YOURSELF AN EXCELLENT M&A ATTORNEY

And speaking of attorneys, surround yourself with the right professionals. This is another stress point for any deal. The wrong attorney will kill it, and I have witnessed the carnage. Attorneys who make their living in real estate or family law, who suddenly step into an M&A deal will kill it with misplaced caution or endless rewrites. Others chip away at trust between buyer and seller, sparring over boiler-plate clauses that seasoned deal lawyers resolve in minutes.

The right attorney is not just a deal-protector; they are a deal-enabler. They know which battles matter and which do not. They protect your downside without poisoning the well. If you remember nothing else about legal help, remember this: hire someone who *does M&A for a living.*

PARALLEL DILIGENCE HAS ITS PLACE
(BUT USUALLY IN LARGER DEALS)

In middle-market and private equity deals, you will often see legal, HR, and compliance tracks run in parallel. There is more money at play, more speed required, and larger teams to manage the moving parts. It makes sense there. But in small to lower-middle market transactions? That's how buyers burn through $100K in professional fees on a deal that never even had a chance.

Holli's Tip: In smaller deals—anything under $15 million—you should put your dollars into financial diligence first. If the numbers do not hold up, you can walk away before the lawyers ever sharpen their pencils. In larger deals—$15 million and above—running legal and financial diligence on parallel tracks can make sense, but only if you are well-capitalized and prepared to absorb the added fees, even if the deal ultimately falls apart.

HOLLI-ISM

Think of diligence like dating: confirm that your date is who they say they are *before* you buy the engagement ring. Otherwise, you are paying for champagne, tux rentals, and photographers for a wedding that never makes it to "I do."

YOU SHOULD NOT GO IT ALONE

Diligence is not a solo sport. You can be very sharp and have read about deals but if you walk into diligence without seasoned help, you are asking for unnecessary risk and big problems.

For buyers: bring in transaction-savvy advisors early, even before the LOI is signed. An advisor who lives and breathes deals can spot red flags that you will miss, test the seller's story before you drink the Kool-Aid, and help you shape terms that actually protect you. They do not just keep you from overpaying—they raise your odds of actually getting to closing.

For sellers: picture sitting across the table from eight buy-side professionals—attorneys, accountants, tax advisors, HR specialists, and consultants—all poking holes in your story. If you walk in alone, you are outnumbered before you start. Sellers need their own team of qualified advisors who can defend the narrative, plug gaps before the buyer finds them, and make sure your legacy (and your value) is not shredded in the process.

M&A is never just numbers. It is money, yes, but it is also stories, reputations, and sometimes the work of a lifetime. That is too much to shoulder by yourself.

FULL DILIGENCE = RISK DISCOVERY

Financial diligence might be the first gatekeeper, but full diligence is where every corner of the business gets turned over. The QofE confirms whether EBITDA is real. Full diligence asks: "What about everything else?"

> IF YOU WALK INTO DILIGENCE WITHOUT SEASONED HELP, YOU ARE ASKING FOR UNNECESSARY RISK AND BIG PROBLEMS.

When diligence begins, the buyer's team isn't just glancing at numbers. They're pulling the entire business apart, piece by piece, to see if it will hold together once they own it. Lawyers comb through entity records and contracts, looking for loose ends or litigation waiting to surface.

Tax experts scour filings, hunting for unpaid exposure or the shadow of an audit. HR pulls employee agreements, PTO liabilities, and benefit obligations—the little grenades that detonate after closing if no one notices them.

Compliance gets its turn: licenses, permits, and regulatory filings that determine whether the business is even allowed to operate tomorrow. Insurance is stripped down to coverage levels and claims history, because nothing screams regret like an uninsured lawsuit. Technology is tested for hidden risks: outdated systems, shaky licenses, or a lurking cybersecurity issue. And then operations—the beating heart of the business—gets stress-tested. Who are the key vendors? Are customers concentrated in too few hands? How much leverage does the other side of the table actually hold?

This is diligence in the real world. It's not paperwork for paperwork's sake—it's a cavity search on a living company, done before the buyer writes the check. For sellers, it's the reminder that clean records, clear contracts, and credible systems aren't "nice-to-haves"—they're the currency that keeps value from slipping away.

SUGGESTED DILIGENCE SEQUENCE

Not sure where to begin? This is the general flow I recommend—especially when capital is limited or risk feels high:

1. **Financial First:** Begin with a preliminary review of the seller's P&L, balance sheet, and tax returns. If concerns emerge, hold off legal spend until risks are addressed.
2. **QofE / Financial Validation**: Engage a QofE provider or financial expert to verify EBITDA, review customer concentration, and test normalization adjustments.
3. **Legal & Operational Review**: Once financials check out, begin reviewing legal contracts, vendor agreements, employment issues, licenses, and compliance.
4. **HR, Tech, & Final Risk Review**: Finalize people-related diligence (PTO liabilities, employee handbooks, benefits) and assess IT systems, insurance, and data security risks.

WHAT IF I HAVE A SMALL DEAL?

Yes—you still do diligence. Deal size doesn't matter. You do not get a hall pass on diligence just because the purchase price has fewer zeroes. You still need to know what you're buying because your goal is to then scale it.

Think of it like this: you don't need a 200-page report with dashboards and glossy charts, but you *do* need to lift the hood. And you'd better bring someone along who knows what to look for. A good advisor can run a limited-scope diligence process that fits the size of the deal without bleeding you dry.

At minimum, you want to see the story unfold over three years—tax returns, full financials (P&L plus balance sheets), and at least 12 to 24 months of bank statements. You want to know how money actually moves, not just how it looks on a broker's spreadsheet.

Then dig into the guts: accounts receivable aging, customer concentration, and the seller's add-back schedule. Do not just take their word for it—have someone walk through the add-backs with you. Get the employee roster, see who's actually keeping the business running, and check comp levels. Review key customer and vendor contracts, debt schedules, any legal filings, licenses, and insurance policies.

Does it feel like overkill for a *small deal*? It's not. A six-figure mistake hurts just as much as a seven-figure one. The size of the check does not change the need for clarity—it just changes how big the flashlight is that you shine on the books. Skipping diligence because the deal is small is like skipping a home inspection because of the size of the house. Guess what? The roof still leaks and still costs a fortune.

WHY DEALS DIE IN DILIGENCE

It happens in predictable ways. A seller springs a surprise they "forgot" to mention. Revenue starts sliding mid-diligence, and suddenly the projections feel more like wishful thinking. Buyers discover customer churn that was conveniently left out of the narrative. Add-backs that looked generous on the Confidential Information Memorandum (CIM) get exposed as inflated. And then there's the slow grind—death by a thousand cuts—where every "small issue" piles up until the buyer's gut just says: *this doesn't feel safe anymore.* Want to see those red flags in living color? There's an entire chapter on this coming up!

> A SIX-FIGURE MISTAKE HURTS JUST AS MUCH AS A SEVEN-FIGURE ONE.

"THE BANK APPROVED IT" MYTH

"Well, the bank approved it, so we must be good."

No. Sorry. Absolutely not.

Banks underwrite loans, not operations. Their job is to make sure the collateral and cash flow pencil out on paper. They are not in the business of telling you whether the business model is broken, the culture is toxic, or the customers are already halfway out the door.

When things go sideways, the bank isn't sending in a rescue team. They assume you, the buyer, will figure it out. Which means you, not the bank, own every problem when the machine starts to break.

THE DISCIPLINE TO WALK

This is where discipline separates the empire builders from the deal chasers.

For buyers, discipline looks like walking away when the risks don't justify the price . . .walking when critical disclosures are withheld . . . walking when the surprises keep stacking until your gut tells you this will cost more than it's worth.

For sellers, discipline is just as important. You can walk when buyers retrade unfairly, when they drown you in unreasonable diligence requests, or when it becomes clear they don't respect your legacy. Walking is power.

THE BOTTOM LINE

Diligence is not a paperwork exercise. It's not box-checking. It is the crucible where both sides earn the right to close.

Buyers: your job is to verify the machine will run once you own it. That means bringing in experts early, asking hard questions, and not being afraid to walk.

Sellers: your job is to prepare the machine to be verified. Every ounce of prep increases buyer confidence, raises valuation, and makes it more likely your deal will cross the finish line.

Every deal carries risk, but the goal is always the same—maximize value and minimize regret.

A downloadable Integration Checklist with "steps for diligence" is in your toolbox available via the QR code at the end of this book.

CHAPTER 12

EARNOUTS-MARRIAGE, DIVORCE, AND EVERYTHING IN BETWEEN

THE HOPE CLAUSE THAT COMES WITH HANDCUFFS

The seller stood by the window of his old office. It was no longer his—the new GM's initials were on the desk. He sold the business three months ago. The check had cleared. His name, removed from the door. It felt like a divorce. Sort of. And yet, every decision of the business still ran through him. The buyer was "supportive"—but distant. The marketing budget was frozen. His top sales rep had been reassigned. Corporate was pushing through new software costs. The earnout clock was ticking. But the levers were no longer really his to pull.

He stared through the glass, earnout slipping through his fingers.

In the distance, a falcon circled the blue sky.

Wild. Decisive. Unbound. Everything he used to be.

Welcome to the emotional reality of a poorly managed earnout.

WHAT IS AN EARNOUT?

An earnout is a fancy M&A term for contingent compensation to the seller—extra payment tied to future performance. It's not a bonus. It's not guaranteed. And it's not free. It's a way for a seller to earn more if certain conditions are met. And for a buyer, it's a tool to de-risk the price by tying future value to actual delivery.

Earnouts aren't evil, but they're dangerous. They need structure, clarity, and discipline—or you won't get paid and that will be another sad seller story out in the marketplace. Earnouts get a bad rap for a reason—plenty of sellers will tell you stories of not getting paid. I will share one of those examples.

But here's the other side of the coin: in my own deals, I've paid most earnouts. Why? Because we set them up with my earnout framework: control, clarity, and cadence. When sellers hit the targets, they got paid. When they didn't, they already knew why—no surprises, no drama. I never had an angry seller sitting across from me as a new employee. They knew it wasn't corporate trickery; it was simply math. That's the difference when you structure earnouts properly.

EARNOUTS: HOPE, HANDCUFFS, AND THE 3 Cs

Earnouts are hope dressed up as math. With handcuffs. I have heard of more than one earnout that began with smiles, champagne toasts, and promises of partnership but ended with lawsuits, bitterness, and one side feeling completely cheated. Like a bad marriage. Sellers are convinced they will crush their numbers. Buyers are convinced the earnout is free upside. The problem? Without control, clarity, and cadence, hope doesn't cash the check.

WHY USE EARNOUTS

Most sellers believe their business is worth more than the buyer believes it is worth. The seller has been wearing hope goggles from the start and the number they carry in their head feels completely justified. Buyers, on the other hand, come in armed with diligence, wanting to get the best possible value. They see risk where the seller sees resilience. They don't trust projections; they trust patterns. That gap between what the seller believes and what the buyer is willing to pay is exactly the type of tension an earnout is designed to resolve.

Sometimes the issue is timing. A seller swears new revenue is just around the corner—a big contract about to be signed, a new product about to launch. The buyer is willing to *believe*... but not willing to *pay* upfront for something

> EARNOUTS ARE HOPE DRESSED UP AS MATH. WITH HANDCUFFS.

that doesn't exist yet. Sometimes the issue is history. Growth in the past doesn't line up with the rosy forecast in the deck. Other times it's simply uncertainty: customer concentration, leadership transition, a market shift no one can quite model.

In all of these cases, the earnout becomes the bridge. It says: "We'll pay you for the future you're so sure about—but only if it actually happens." For the buyer, it's risk mitigation. For the seller, it's a shot at the upside they believe they've already earned.

At its core, the earnout exists because valuation is rarely a math problem. It's a trust problem. And the earnout is the structure that allows two sides with different versions of the truth to still find a way forward.

WHERE EARNOUTS GO WRONG

Everyone loves to say: "We both want the earnout to be paid." It sounds so wholesome, almost like a wedding vow. But then the honeymoon ends, lawyers get involved, and suddenly no one is smiling. And the seller is left staring at a zero. So why does this keep happening?

At the root, it usually comes down to three killers: lack of control, unclear metrics, and what I call *accidental sabotage.*

Let's start with control. Earnouts fail when sellers are expected to hit numbers without any real authority to make the calls that drive those numbers. Imagine being told to win the race while someone else has the keys to the car. That is not performance; that's a setup.

Then there's the issue of clarity. Earnout metrics are often vague or loaded with assumptions. "EBITDA target," for example, sounds clean on paper. But in reality? It's a playground for interpretation. What counts as an add-back? Whose version of the P&L are we using? How are corporate allocations handled? Will the Balance Sheet be involved? If the seller can't recite the metric in a single breath, it is probably too fuzzy to be enforceable. And don't even get me started on earnout's using GAAP and throwing around accounting terminology no seller truly knows. And by the way, neither does your attorney–they expect the business people to make sure these definitions are okay.

And finally—sabotage. Rarely intentional, but deadly all the same. Picture this: a seller nails year one, then corporate parachutes in. Suddenly there's new accounting software to implement, a training program that eats up billable hours, new managers with six-figure salaries, and overhead that never existed before. EBITDA tanks, not because the business didn't perform but the rules of the game changed midstream.

That's the heartbreak of a poorly written earnout: the outcome is never really in the seller's hands.

A well-built earnout is not just a clause in the contract. It is discipline on both sides. (There's that word again.) Done right, it creates alignment. And if the seller does not hit the numbers? Then there is no drama, no finger-pointing, no courtroom—just math.

As a buyer, I love earnouts. I used them as a tool to bridge the gap between what a seller believed their business was worth and what the financials actually supported. It is a performance-based structure that gives both parties a path forward.

Every earnout that succeeds has three things in common. Without them? You are setting yourself up for lawsuits, resentment, and late-night phone calls to lawyers you never wanted to meet. Hope is fine for lottery tickets. But if you are putting millions on the line? You want control, clarity, and cadence every single time.

HOLLI'S 3 Cs OF EARNOUTS™

- **Control**-Who holds the levers that drive the performance metrics?
- **Clarity**-Are the targets, timelines, and mechanics spelled out with little wiggle room?
- **Cadence**-How often is progress measured and communicated so no one wakes up surprised in year three?

CONTROL

If the seller cannot actually pull the levers to ensure success, then the earnout is already broken. Revenue-based earnout? The seller needs authority over pricing, sales strategy, and the customers who drive those numbers. EBITDA-based earnout? The seller must be able to manage staffing, expenses, pricing, and margins.

Take away those levers, and the earnout is just a cruel joke. Imagine telling someone they'll be rewarded for driving across town—but you took away the car keys. That is how most earnout fights begin.

CLARITY

Earnouts implode because people fail to define the target. If it is EBITDA, on the surface, EBITDA looks clean and universal—the "king" of deal metrics. If the target is revenue, you would think that is even easier to define. But all targets bend under the weight of accounting choices.

Ask yourself:

- *Is that new hire a one-time growth cost or a recurring expense?*
- *Are software development costs expensed or capitalized?*
- *Does bad debt come off Revenue or EBITDA, or is it considered extraordinary?*
- *How are integration costs handled—seller's responsibility or the buyer's choice?*

Each answer swings EBITDA or revenue. And in an earnout, even a swing of a few hundred thousand dollars can decide whether the seller gets paid—or walks away empty-handed.

Once PE or a strategic buyer takes control, they may push down *their* costs into *your* business. And the shiny new general manager they install at a six-figure salary? It comes straight out of "your" EBITDA. The enterprise-grade accounting software that costs five times what you were paying? It gets booked against your earnout target. Overnight, your carefully negotiated deal economics are eaten alive by decisions you no longer control.

That's why, in every earnout, the target must be defined in *painstaking* detail. Line by line. Expense by expense. Assume nothing. Spell out what counts and what doesn't. If your agreement just says, "EBITDA as defined by GAAP," you've written yourself an invitation to court.

> IN EVERY EARNOUT, THE TARGET MUST BE DEFINED IN PAINSTAKING DETAIL.

Many agreements try to guard against disputes with the phrase: "EBITDA shall be calculated in accordance with GAAP and consistent with the company's historical practices." Even when both sides agree to "GAAP and historical practice," there's still wiggle room. Why? Because GAAP itself allows judgment calls—estimates that can be conservative or aggressive depending on who is making them. Take bad debt reserves: GAAP requires you to estimate what portion of receivables won't be collected. One seller might carry a 2% reserve, while a more cautious buyer's accountant might say it should be 8%. Both are "GAAP compliant," but that swing alone could shave hundreds of thousands off EBITDA.

Other examples:

- **Warranty reserves**—aggressive vs. conservative assumptions

- **Capitalization thresholds**—Do you expense a $5,000 software build, or capitalize it? Both can be "reasonable."
- **Inventory obsolescence**—What gets written off and when?

So even if you've nailed down "GAAP plus historical practice," you may still be negotiating in a fog of estimates. That's why the earnout definition must not just say "in accordance with GAAP," but specify how estimates, reserves, and thresholds will be treated.

Instead of relying on "historical practice," nail down clarity in writing:

- **List inclusions and exclusions.** No corporate allocations. No new management salaries. No software amortization beyond what existed pre-close.
- **Require mutual consent.** Any deviation from the baseline must be agreed in writing.
- **Guard against GAAP gray zones.** Even "clean GAAP" leaves room for interpretation. Bad debt reserves, warranty reserves, capitalization thresholds—these all come down to management judgment. Without tight definitions, the buyer can "lean conservative" and crush earnout targets.
- **Ban corporate push downs.** Spell out that holding company costs, integration costs, or shared services cannot be pushed into the target's P&L unless both sides consent.
- **Reference schedules if possible.** Attach a sample EBITDA build from the seller's audited year as an exhibit. That way, the methodology is memorialized, not just the words.
- **Add dispute mechanics.** Define what happens if there's disagreement (e.g., an independent accountant resolves

disputes at the buyer's expense). Sellers often skip this, but it's your last line of defense.

Vagueness equals value leakage. And in earnouts, value leakage almost always flows away from the seller.

CADENCE

An earnout should never be a "set it and forget it" clause buried in the purchase agreement. It must be tracked, reviewed, and communicated in real time. That means monthly or quarterly reviews, not a surprise two years later when everyone suddenly discovers the target was missed.

Cadence is about rhythm. Scheduled meetings. Sellers must see the numbers tied to their earnout, otherwise they are flying blind. And nothing breeds conflict faster than surprise. When you weave together control, clarity, and cadence, you create what I call earnout harmony where both buyer and seller know the rules, track the progress, and avoid the courtroom.

HOLLI'S RULES FOR EARNOUTS

A few more ground rules for your purchase agreement from the trenches:

- If you're the seller: push for no cap. You want unlimited upside if you blow past the targets.
- If you're the buyer: cap it. Tie the payout to real growth that moves the business forward, not just lucky timing.
- Get every detail in writing—not just "agreed to," but fully spelled out in the purchase agreement.

- Define all metrics with surgical precision. Especially revenue and EBITDA.
- Bake in reporting rights. Sellers should be entitled to regular updates and even quarterly meetings, whether virtual or in person, to track performance and raise disputes before they turn into litigation.
- And here's the big one for sellers: ask for an acceleration clause. That way, if you hit certain milestones early, or if you're terminated without cause, the earnout pays out in full. It is your protection against being pushed out before the clock runs down.

> EARNOUTS ARE SUPPOSED TO ALIGN INTERESTS. WITHOUT RULES, THEY BREED CONFLICT.

Earnouts are supposed to align interests. Without rules, they breed conflict. With structure, they can actually work—but only if both sides are disciplined enough to honor the 3 Cs.

THE DEFINITION THAT SAVED MILLIONS

One time, I worked with a client who scored an eight-figure exit. I had been side by side with him and his team from the moment we began preparing the company for sale. I was there through every negotiation, every redline of the legal documents, and every meeting with the private equity buyer. When it came time to hammer out the details of the earnout, the stakes were high.

The earnout was based on two things: revenue and gross margin percentage. Straightforward, right? Except revenue was defined as *revenue less bad debt*. That little phrase "less bad debt" had the power to make or break the entire earnout.

Most sellers skim past a line like that. My client even asked, "Is this really a big deal?" My answer: "Yep. Huge." Because under GAAP, bad debt is just an estimate. Estimates leave room for interpretation. And in M&A, interpretation is where the fights live. *Who is doing the estimating? Are they ultra-conservative? Conveniently aggressive?* The definition as written—"bad debt as historically calculated in accordance with GAAP" was fog in a distant horizon.

I applied one of 3 Cs right there. For clarity, I drafted a tight definition that left no wiggle room. Bad debt would *not* include amounts past due but subject to ongoing collection efforts, amounts in dispute but unresolved, or anything uncollected because of the buyer's own actions or omissions after closing. That language was painstakingly detailed—and it mattered.

Three months post-close, my client saw exactly why. The private equity group rolled out their own aggressive bad debt policy. Suddenly, invoices we would have reasonably collected were being written off. They also changed how we invoiced insurance-paying clients, which predictably drove up bad debt even further. My client's earnout was at risk, not because of performance, but because of accounting treatment.

But we had the language. We went back to the purchase agreement, pulled out the section I had insisted on, and sat down with the attorney. Our counsel agreed: the buyer had to comply with our definition, not theirs. We met with the PE group, and they conceded. The earnout stood. That one clause protected literally millions of dollars.

This is why you do not skim definitions! This is why you apply the 3 Cs with discipline. And this is why you bring in experts who know how to find the small details that can turn into huge problems. What looks like a foot-note can decide whether your earnout pays—or evaporates.

NEW BUYERS COME UP WITH THE WORST EARNOUTS

I hate to say it, but some of the worst earnouts come from new buyers. Fresh buyers often get creative in the wrong ways. They tie small dollars to meaningless goals, or worse—they design earnouts that let the seller back-slide and still walk away with nearly the whole pot.

Here's the problem: revenue can fall, EBITDA can cra-ter, and yet the seller still cashes the check. Meanwhile, the buyer is left holding debt they can no longer ser-vice. That is not a partnership. That is a disaster in slow motion.

I once saw a buyer structure an earnout that bit him right in the *you-know-where*. The deal was about $950K, and the seller could still collect 95% of their earnout even if revenue dropped 15%. Think about that. The seller had zero incentive to grow, and every incentive to ride it out, take their check, and move on. The buyer? They were stuck trying to make loan payments on a shrinking busi-ness. Ouch.

This is what happens when buyers forget what their long-term goal actually is. If you want to grow EBITDA, do not tie the seller to revenue alone. Revenue is the eas-iest number in the world to game—just slash prices or offer discounts and the top line looks great. But margin collapses, cash flow shrinks, and suddenly that business you thought was expanding is bleeding out.

Earnouts should drive alignment. They should push the seller to grow the business in the same direction the buyer wants it to go. If they do not? The buyer will pay dearly for their own sloppy structure.

SCENARIO PLANNING: STRESS TESTING THE EARNOUT

Scenario planning is reality for sophisticated buyers. It is the stress test. You are not trying to be psychic. You are trying to figure out, before you sign, who is happy, who is angry, and who is threatening to sue if things do not go exactly as planned. So how do you do that? You run three plays:

Base Case—the Pretty Version: This is what everyone *thinks* will happen. Use the seller's forecast or something just a little more conservative. Ask: *does the seller actually hit the full earnout? Can the buyer comfortably pay it without choking cash flow?* If not, that's a red flag.

Worst Case—the Gut Punch: *What happens if a key client leaves? Or if pricing pressure cuts into margin?* Suddenly EBITDA slides. Ask: does the seller still walk away with most of the earnout while the buyer is underwater on debt service? If yes, the earnout is broken.

Best Case—Champagne Problems: Let's say revenue shoots past forecast and margins fatten. Sounds great. But *is there a cap?* If there is, *does the seller feel like they got punished for overperforming?* Nothing tanks goodwill faster than a seller who feels robbed of upside they earned.

WHY THIS MATTERS

Scenario planning is not about predicting the future perfectly. It is about making sure your earnout is tied to the right behaviors. If you tie it only to revenue, sellers may drop price and chase volume—while EBITDA tanks.

If you tie it to EBITDA but let the buyer stuff in corporate overhead, sellers will never have a fair shot.

Done right, scenario planning answers three questions clearly:

1. Does this structure align with the buyer's growth strategy?
2. Does it support sustainable cash flow, not just a fantasy model?
3. Does it reward the behavior we actually want to incentivize?

If the structure rewards the wrong outcomes, you may end up with a seller who feels cheated or a buyer who can't afford the business they just bought. No one wins in that situation.

PSYCHOLOGY OF THE EARNOUT

Sellers: Let's be honest, saying yes to an earnout means saying yes to being an employee again. Are you emotionally ready for that?

This is where so many founders stumble. They feel like owners, but the ink on the purchase agreement says otherwise. Suddenly, the company that was "theirs" for years now belongs to someone else even if there is rollover equity. Decisions no longer begin and end with them. And yet, the earnout requires them to perform as if they're still in charge—without actually being in charge.

Professional buyers bring discipline with them. That means GAAP accounting comes front and center. And GAAP has no patience for the shortcuts that small businesses love. Suddenly:

- Employees must submit expense reports on time.
- Jobs have to be closed promptly, with percentage completed recorded.
- Subcontractor invoices must be in before month-end.
- Accruals matter. Timing matters. Every detail matters.

Here's the deal: you could miss your earnout not because you failed to grow, but because someone didn't turn in paperwork.

If you want to survive the psychology of an earnout, you have to embrace discipline, alignment, and a willingness to operate like a partner—not an owner. The mindset shift is everything.

SELLER MINDSET CHECKLIST: ARE YOU READY FOR THE EARNOUT?

Think of this as your gut-check. If you answer "no" to any of these, stop and reassess before signing:

- I understand I am no longer the owner—I will be reporting to someone else.
- I know the earnout is not guaranteed, and I am emotionally prepared if I never see that check.
- I can work within a structured, GAAP-compliant environment.
- I am willing to submit documentation, justify expenses, and meet deadlines without resentment.
- I want to collaborate, not control.
- I have reviewed the deal terms with a tax and legal advisor—and I was not afraid to ask "dumb" questions.
- I understand exactly how my earnout is tracked—and how often I'll see those numbers.

If you cannot confidently check these boxes, pause. Clarity now saves pain later. Better to ask the tough questions today than to live in resentment tomorrow.

REAL STORIES FROM THE M&A BATTLEFIELD

Earnouts look neat on paper. In practice? They're messy, human, and often unpredictable. I've lived through every version of them—the clever, the careless, and the heartbreaking.

One time, I represented a seller in a sizable transaction with private equity. On the surface, the earnout was simple: revenue targets with a gross margin floor. The problem? The seller already operated above that floor. The structure unintentionally encouraged him to chase low margin work just to pump revenue. I flagged it. The buyer realized the trap they had set for themselves. It delayed the deal, but it saved everyone from a structure that rewarded the wrong behavior.

Another time, I worked with a family office who was rolling up accounting firms. Their earnout tied only to flat revenue—no "teeth" in the deal. No incentive to control costs or grow EBITDA. I suggested they tie it to gross margin instead—something that aligned with both growth and profitability. They agreed, and suddenly both sides had skin in the right game.

And finally, a story I wish had ended differently. A small professional services firm, a founder gone too soon, and a partner left grieving. She wanted out quickly, and we closed fast. Too fast. She didn't fully understand the finances or the earnout. She disengaged. The team felt abandoned. The earnout was never paid. That deal still sits heavy with me because it proved a truth I carry into every negotiation: grief doesn't negotiate well.

Earnouts aren't just numbers on a page—they're levers tied to behavior, incentives, and real people. When they're structured poorly, they create frustration and mistrust. When they're designed thoughtfully, they align interests, create clarity, and give both sides a fair shot at success.

BOTTOM LINE

Earnouts are not evil. But they're not magic either. They're a tool—and tools only work if you use them right. If you want to protect the millions, then define the terms with clarity, give control to the people who can move the levers, and set a cadence for tracking that keeps everyone aligned in real time.

That's how you maximize value and minimize regret.

CHAPTER 13

COVER YOUR . . . TAIL INSURANCE

THE CLAUSE NO ONE TALKS ABOUT
UNTIL IT'S TOO LATE

In a dimly lit conference room just outside of Boston, the deal came to life. Papers were signed and everyone leaned back with that rare sigh of relief that comes when years of work finally meet their payday. On the surface, it was the picture of a clean exit.

But six months later, the illusion shattered. The buyer's phone lit up with the kind of call no one wants: a lawsuit. The claim reached back into the seller's tenure, but the insurance policy that once offered protection lapsed at closing. The coverage was gone. The liability was real. Overnight, what looked like a smooth handoff became a financial and legal disaster.

Who is liable in this case? Buyer or seller? Well, let me hand the mic to Oprah, "YOU get a lawsuit, and YOU get a lawsuit! And YOU get a lawsuit! Yes, congratulations EVERYONE gets a lawsuit!"

Unless . . .you cover your tail.

Tail insurance isn't a game. It's not fun, exciting, or anything you can pin on a donkey. However, if you don't have it, the game becomes pin the lawsuit on the donkey—and you're not the one doing the pinning.

Tail insurance is rarely talked about in M&A and most people don't even know it exists. It doesn't show up on glossy deal decks or make it into celebratory LinkedIn posts.

But it's the invisible shield that keeps both buyer and seller safe when old liabilities come knocking. As exciting and necessary as a smoke detector—boring, easy to forget, but also the only thing standing between you and disaster at 3:00 a.m.

Now, because the only subject more boring than accounting is insurance, let's have another Mock-Tale!

THE SMART UMBRELLA

Picture this: It's the company's big closing day. The deal is signed, and everyone is headed outside to the beautiful park across the street for a celebratory soiree and "family" photos under a bright blue sky. Enter Patrick, the CFO, holding a giant golf umbrella.

"Hey Pat," someone scoffs, "You look ridiculous. It's sunny. Put that thing away."

But Patrick just shrugs. "You never know."

Fast forward twenty minutes. The champagne buzz is rolling in with the clouds, and suddenly it's a Texas-style downpour. Everyone's drenched, makeup running, suits ruined, LinkedIn photos are postponed indefinitely. Everyone except Patrick—cool, dry, sipping a mimosa happily under his golf umbrella.

That's tail coverage. Most people roll their eyes when you bring it up. It feels bulky, boring, and unnecessary—until the storm hits. Then the one who covered their tail walks away looking like the smartest one in the room.

TAIL COVERAGE EXPLAINED

Tail insurance—also known as extended reporting coverage—is not a new policy. It's an extension of an existing claims-made policy such as:

- E&O (Errors and Omissions)
- D&O (Directors and Officers)
- Cyber Liability
- EPLI (Employment Practices Liability Insurance)
- Malpractice

These policies on their own only cover claims that are both made and reported while the policy is active. Once the seller cancels their policy post-close, they're exposed—and this is why you buy a tail. Tail coverage ensures those old policies still respond to claims made *after* the deal closes, for actions that happened *before* it did.

> TAIL INSURANCE IS RARELY TALKED ABOUT IN M&A AND MOST PEOPLE DON'T EVEN KNOW IT EXISTS.

In M&A, tail insurance means the seller's professional liability or E&O coverage doesn't just stop on closing day—it extends into the future to cover claims from their past operations. Buyers sleep better. Sellers protect their legacy. Deals close cleaner.

- **Occurrence-based policies (like general liability):** Coverage is tied to when the event happened. If the incident occurred during the policy period, you're covered—even if the claim is filed years later. For example, a slip-and-fall in 2020 would still be covered by the 2020 policy.

- **Claims-made policies (like E&O, D&O, EPLI, malpractice):** Coverage is stricter. Two conditions must be met: (1) the incident occurred during the policy period, and (2) the claim was filed during that same period. Once the policy expires, no new claims are covered—even if the event happened earlier.

That's why tail insurance matters in M&A. When a seller cancels a claims-made policy at closing, they're exposed. The business may have changed hands, but old liabilities can surface months or years later. Without a tail, the buyer inherits those risks, and the seller's "clean exit" can quickly turn into a legal mess.

COVER YOUR ASSETS

Now, you might be wondering, *Do I need tail insurance for an asset deal?* The answer is emphatically—yes. Period. No ifs, ands, or buts about it—cover your assets! And before you ask "what about reps, warranties, indemnifications," and all that other legal mumbo jumbo—the answer is no—it cannot and does not protect you fully.

Let's keep going.

Buyers love to believe an asset deal is a magic shield. "We only bought the assets, not the liabilities." Sounds good in theory. But courts don't just look at paperwork—they look at reality. If you kept the employees, customers, systems, and brand, guess what? You likely bought the liabilities too. At the very least, you got the keys to a brand-new lawsuit and you will spend valuable time and resources defending your innocence if you don't cover your tail.

This is why tail insurance exists. It's the safety net under the tightrope. Because indemnifications in your purchase agreement sound good, but when claims sur-face years later, enforcing them can be slow, messy, and expensive.

Most first-time buyers—and even a surprising number of seasoned ones—think tail insurance only matters in stock deals. Not true. Liability doesn't always follow the form of the deal. I learned this early from one of my men-tors, Frank, a board member and investment banker who had been through hundreds of transactions. He drilled it into me, "Always have the seller get tail insurance—even in asset deals." And he was right. Frank was always right.

Smart buyers insist on it. Smart sellers should too. And the true M&A masters? They don't care if it's stock or asset, big deal or small—they always get tail coverage.

WHY SELLERS SHOULD ALWAYS GET TAIL INSURANCE

Even in a stock sale where the legal entity techni-cally lives on, sellers are not off the hook. If something happened on your watch, it could still come back to you. Breach of duty claims, client disputes, employment law-suits—they don't vanish with a closing signature. They just wait for their moment.

And once the deal closes, you no longer control the defense. The buyer chooses the legal strategy, the lawyers, even whether you are informed. They may swap insurance carriers, or worse, drop coverage altogether. Without tail insurance, you could find yourself standing alone in front of a claim with no shield.

For sellers, tail insurance is essential and is peace of mind. It is the difference between walking away with a clean exit and lying awake at night wondering if an old employee complaint will surface years later. It's a one-time premium to protect years of your work and your financial future.

WHY BUYERS SHOULD REQUIRE IT– EVEN IN ASSET DEALS

Buyers often assume asset deals are safe from old liabilities. As stated earlier, courts look at substance, not form. If you keep the employees, the customers, the brand, and the systems—guess what? You may have bought the liability too—and you didn't even know it.

Post-close claims are common. A customer sues over a project completed last quarter. A former employee brings a harassment claim. You're the new owner, which makes you the first target. Indemnification clauses? They're nice, but if the seller dissolves or spends their payout, good luck collecting. Defense costs alone can cripple a deal.

> REMEMBER, TAIL INSURANCE ISN'T A BRAND NEW POLICY, IT'S AN EXTENSION.

That's why seasoned buyers require tail coverage. It protects the investment the same way reps and warranties do. It keeps the exit clean. And it saves the buyer from burning cash on old ghosts they never signed up for.

BUT DO M&A EXPERTS ACTUALLY REQUIRE THIS?

If an M&A expert really knows what they are doing, they will absolutely require this. If they don't, I would count that as a red flag. Tail insurance isn't some fringe idea whispered about by over-cautious lawyers. It's standard in smart deals: SBA-backed transactions, private equity, institutional investors, and bank-financed acquisitions. The pros check the box every time. Choose the experts who are looking out for your best interest, not just theirs.

When tail insurance gets skipped, it's usually for one of two reasons: someone is trying to save money, or they simply don't know it exists. Both are dangerous. The "savings" vanish the moment a claim shows up.

Most tail coverage runs three to six years. My advice? Push for six. Why? Because I don't like surprises—especially the kind that arrive in the mail with a court date.

A REAL STORY: WHY TAIL INSURANCE MATTERS

I was working with a client on a roll-up, and I insisted the seller obtain tail insurance. We didn't just talk about it—we required it in the asset purchase agreement. It was a condition of closing that the seller provide the certificate.

Fast forward a few weeks: I was on-site with the client, meeting the staff and beginning integration. One of the first steps I take is to sit down with every single employee. On the very last interview of the day, an employee started talking about a potential lawsuit. They had already consulted with counsel.

I looked at the buyer, and we both knew what that meant.

"Thank God we required tail insurance!"

COST AND LOGISTICS

Remember, tail insurance is not a brand-new policy. It's an extension. You don't shop around for it like car insurance. It comes directly from the carrier that wrote the original policy. It's a one-time premium, often calculated as a multiple of the expiring annual premium. Think of it like pre-paying for peace of mind. You write one check, and the past stays protected. Who pays for tail? Most of the time, the seller. But like everything else in M&A, it's negotiable. The trick is to get it quoted early—ask your broker before the deal papers are signed so there are no last-minute surprises.

REAL-WORLD WAKE-UP CALL

This is not just theory. Courts are willing, today, to look past the form of your deal if the substance says otherwise. The following court case, Campbell v. WeCare Organics, LLC (Pa. Super. Ct. 2024), is a wake-up call because it shows that courts are willing to pierce the asset-sale shield if the deal looks too much like a continuation or merger.

Campbell, a hauling service, was owed over $120K by WeCare. Before paying, WeCare sold its assets to Denali Water Solutions. Campbell sued Denali, arguing successor liability—saying basically, "You bought the business, you bought the problem." The court agreed. Even though it was structured as an *asset deal*, the transaction looked enough like a merger that Denali got dragged into the liability.

Tail insurance would not have prevented the lawsuit itself however, it would have provided a legal defense and coverage—a buffer between Denali and an expensive surprise.

TAIL INSURANCE AT-A-GLANCE

What It Is:
An extension of an existing claims-made policy (not a brand-new policy).

Applies To:
E&O, D&O, Cyber Liability, EPLI, Malpractice.

Does Not Apply To:
General Liability (CGL)—usually occurrence-based, so it already covers past events.

Why It Matters:
Keeps the door shut on liabilities that happened before the sale but surface afterward.

Who Should Get It:
The seller—it protects against past liabilities long after you walk away.

Who Requires It:
Smart buyers, SBA lenders, banks, private equity, institutional investors.

Typical Duration:
3–6 years (pick 6 if you want to sleep at night).

Cost:
One-time fee, usually 2–3x the expiring annual premium.

Where to Get It:
Usually from the same carrier who wrote the original policy.

Who Pays:
Usually the seller (but negotiable—bake it into the deal).

BOTTOM LINE

Tail insurance is not about trust—it is about wisdom. It is the final bow on the seller's clean exit and the buyer's first layer of protection.

In M&A, the missing millions are not only found in EBITDA adjustments or earnout terms. Sometimes they are preserved by something as unglamorous as tail coverage. Quiet details like this are how you *minimize regret in every transaction*—and that, more than anything, is the ultimate return.

CHAPTER 14

LONG LIVE THE HUMANS—
THE HANDOFF

TAKING CARE OF THE PEOPLE WHO MAKE IT ALL WORK

The conference room smelled like coffee, donuts, and stress. The thirty or so staff members huddled in silence— some sitting, some lining the wall. A few scrolling on their phones.

Swallowing his last bite of cream puff, Bob from maintenance licked his fingers and blurted, "Are we getting laid off?"

Sharon, from the front desk gasped.

Chad from sales dropped his head in disbelief.

Not a soul dared to answer.

At precisely 9:17 a.m. the door swung open. The owner walked in with a suited stranger trailing, "Good morning, everyone. Did you get coffee? And donuts, I see." His voice was too chipper, too practiced—as if the box of pastries could cushion whatever bomb was about to drop. The truth? He hadn't even bought them. It was his secretary's idea.

"Good morning." The half-hearted chorus replied.

The two suits took their place at the head of the room. The owner clasped his hands, cleared his throat, and got straight to the point.

"Well, I've sold the company."

Crickets. No one clapped. Blank stares all around. He

smiled awkwardly, then motioned to the suited stranger beside him. "This is the new buyer, Cliff—Cliff Hanger."

Cliff stepped forward, too eager, too polished.

"I'm excited to meet you all. Don't worry—nothing will change."

And that's when everything changed.

The deal that looked so good on paper had just entered the hardest part: winning over the humans who would make it or break it—holding on for dear life.

WE NEED HUMANS

I've said it from the start—deals are not just spreadsheets and numbers—they are also people. This is where business meets heart. Where deals hit reality. And where the best buyers—and the most honorable sellers—either rise to the occasion or start the slow trickle of millions out the door through turnover, disengagement, and cultural collapse.

Contrary to popular soundbites circulating—there are no self-made millionaires, only *team-made* millionaires. Behind every EBITDA multiple is a team of people who got you there. And those same people will determine whether the buyer ever sees the return they modeled. Integration isn't just operational. It's emotional. You don't integrate balance sheets. You integrate humans—who are worried, skeptical, and scanning for signs of trust or betrayal.

This chapter is about how to carry the deal across the finish line by taking care of the very people who built the value.

TELL THE TRUTH, BUILD THE BRIDGE

Employees can smell half-truths from across the room. The fastest way to lose the trust of the team you just acquired is to offer false comfort or to hide behind corporate phrases. "Nothing will change" might sound reassuring in the moment, but it lands flat. Because something always changes. Reporting lines. PTO policies. The software they log into every morning. Even the titles on their email signatures. Pretending otherwise sets you up for distrust.

Here's a better approach: tell them what *will* change, what you don't know yet, and when they'll hear from you again. It's not weakness; it's credibility. Day one is less about answers and more about showing that you'll be transparent.

> DAY ONE IS LESS ABOUT ANSWERS AND MORE ABOUT SHOWING THAT YOU'LL BE TRANSPARENT.

It happens all the time: a buyer tells the room, "Nothing will change." And then things do. Not necessarily dramatic things— sometimes just policies, titles, or processes. But because employees were promised the opposite, the changes feel like broken trust. *What else is coming that we don't know about?* I've seen it stall momentum in deals that should have been smooth. A single sentence could have changed the trajectory: "Some things will shift. We promise to communicate clearly and quickly."

And sellers—you carry just as much responsibility here. Do not spring a sale on your long-term employees the Friday before the buyer walks in the door on Monday. I watched this unfold with a client. The seller had promised ownership and opportunity to key staff for years. When the truth came out—suddenly, and without warning—the team felt betrayed. They weren't angry at the buyer; they were angry at the person they had trusted. By the time we arrived on-site, emotions were raw, and my client, the buyer, had to help mop up. The irony? The buyer was prepared to invest in them, to give them more career runway than they'd ever had. But in those first days, they couldn't see it through the fog of broken promises.

The lesson: timing and truth matter. Employees don't need perfection. They need honesty.

BUILD A PITCH DECK-SERIOUSLY

Let me be blunt: walking into your first team meeting without a pitch deck is like showing up to the alter without vows. Everyone is waiting to hear what this new future looks like, and "winging it" will not cut it.

A pitch deck is not corporate fluff. Done well, it's your north star. It says: "We've thought about this. We care. And here's where we're headed—together."

That same buyer from the story above walked into a room full of employees just days after the deal closed where the seller had promised ownership opportunities for years but never delivered, and the truth only came out a few days before the sale was closed. During the pitch, the team was stone-faced, silent, and visibly angry. You could have heard a pin drop. After the slides, we sat down with each employee one-on-one, asked why they were upset, and then listened. They felt the owner was looking out for himself without caring for the needs of his loyal employees. After we heard and validated them, only then could we begin rebuilding trust.

That is what a pitch deck should do at scale: give the team something to hold onto in the chaos. Structure the story, answer the obvious questions, and lay out the path forward.

Here's how to shape it:

Title & Tagline
Give the room a headline they can rally around. Something as simple as: *Welcome to Our New Chapter.* Or: *Same Team. Stronger Future.*

Who We Are
Start with you. The buyer. Share your background, your mission, your values. People need to know who just stepped into the captain's seat.

Why We Bought This Company
This is where trust starts. Tell them what you saw in their business. Why you believed it was worth your capital. Why you believe in them.

What Will Change
Do not dance around this one. List it. Be specific. If PTO policies shift, if approval layers are added, if software systems are changing—say it here. Let people brace and adapt.

What Will Stay the Same
This is your chance to calm the room. If their jobs, culture, or leadership structure remain intact, spell that out. People cling to anchors in moments of transition.

Your Questions Answered
The big three always surface: *Will I still have a job? What about my pay? What about my vacation?* Address these head-on. Uncertainty is what breeds hallway rumors.

Opportunities Ahead
Show them what's next. New training. Promotions. Tools. A bigger stage for their talents. Help them see a future, not just a transaction.

Meet the Leadership
Put faces to names. Photos, roles, and contact info. People follow people, not logos.

How to Stay Connected
End by building a bridge. Invite questions. Commit to transparency. Make it clear: the conversation doesn't end with this deck—it begins with it.

> EMPLOYEES EXPERIENCE PTO THROUGH EMOTIONS, NOT SPREADSHEETS.

VACATION/PTO: THE SILENT TRUST BREAKER

In every deal, there are the big headline items—purchase price, working capital, earnouts. And then there are the quiet details that can undo trust in a heartbeat. Vacation or Paid-Time-Off (PTO) is one of them.

In most asset deals, accrued PTO gets paid out at closing by the seller unless the parties agree otherwise. On paper, that sounds tidy. The math checks out. Employees are "made whole." But here's how it lands in real life: An employee opens their paycheck and sees their vacation turned into taxable income. The trip they booked for next month? Suddenly unpaid. No warning, no conversation. What felt like a benefit has been reduced to a transaction. That's the moment you lose them. This isn't about policy—it's about respect. Employees don't care how the purchase agreement reads; they care that their earned time off is recognized and honored.

So, buyers and sellers need to get aligned early. Decide: will vacation/PTO balances carry forward, or will they be cashed out? Put it in writing. And most importantly—communicate it. Not in a throwaway email, not buried in the handbook, but face-to-face, with clarity. Because the truth is, employees experience PTO through emotions, not spreadsheets. This is part of negotiating the unseen we talked about in the very beginning. Handle it well, and you build credibility. Handle it poorly, and you create a silent trust break that can haunt your integration for months.

Here are the deal dynamics:

- In asset sales, it's negotiable. Sellers usually pay it out, but buyers can agree to carry it. Employees feel the difference.
- In stock sales, the liability just rolls over. PTO balances stay intact unless the buyer changes policy later.

The takeaway: in asset deals, PTO is not automatic. Decide early. Communicate clearly. Document the treatment in the closing schedules. Do that, and you protect both your people and your deal.

HOLLI IN THE TRENCHES

I have seen this play out more ways than I can count. It's no fun sitting in rooms where sellers broke promises to their employees. I've seen buyers so focused on the deal model that they forgot the basic question every employee is asking: *What's in it for me?* Silence turned into turnover, and turnover turned into client loss and inefficiency—that cost millions.

I've also lived it myself as a buyer. On paper, we

acquired revenue and relationships. In reality, we inherited years of broken leadership and a demoralized team. That's the unseen. No spreadsheet showed it—until it hit our results, and the cost was undeniable.

Business is money and people. The truth is simple: when you ignore employees, the bill always comes due. It may not show up in diligence, but it will show up in morale, efficiency, and ultimately value. Treat employees the way you would want to be treated—honestly, directly, and with respect for their future. Because no matter how sharp the financial model looks, it is people who make it work.

THE SELLER'S FINAL ACT

Sellers, this isn't your exit. It's your encore.

You've spent years—sometimes decades—building this team. The people in those chairs carried your vision, your headaches, and your late-night emails. They deserve more than a silent disappearing act after the ink dries.

When you emotionally (or physically) "check out" the second the check clears, you leave a leadership vacuum. That vacuum will get filled—with fear, speculation, or bitterness. And that can torch your legacy. So instead of vanishing, give your people the dignity of a thoughtful handoff. Here's how to do it well:

- **Host a thoughtful handoff.** Gather your team with intention, not as an afterthought.
- **Introduce the buyer in your own voice.** Frame the decision around what this means for employees: new opportunities, more resources, stronger stability—not just your personal exit.

- **Show what's in it for them.** Highlight growth paths, training, or benefits the buyer brings. Employees need to see how this move serves *their* future, not just yours.
- **Say thank you.** Make it heartfelt. They carried the business that made this deal possible.

Think of it this way: this is not the end of your leadership. It's the moment you prove to your people that you didn't just cash out—you cared enough to pass the torch with dignity and to leave them in a better place than when you found them.

You built this team. Take the time to exit like a leader, not just a seller.

COMMON BUYER MISTAKES

Buyers: do not stumble or bumble through this important aspect of beginning integration. Here are the most common missteps I see:

- Showing up unprepared.
- Avoiding hard questions.
- Failing to mention compensation, benefits, or title changes.
- Over-promising and under-communicating.

BUYER BEST PRACTICES

The best buyers flip that script. They treat day one like a launch—thoughtful, prepared, and human. Here's how they do it:

- Treat Day One like a launch.
- Bring snacks. Yes, seriously.

- Have HR or you be ready to answer detailed benefit questions.
- Schedule team and one-on-one meetings.
- Keep a standing 30-minute weekly Q&A for 90 days.

This is not overkill. It's integration.

THE BOTTOM LINE

Employees are the oxygen of the business. You cannot scale, innovate, or execute without their trust. When buyers stumble here, the "missing millions" don't come from a miscalculated EBITDA or a sloppy working capital peg—they vanish quietly through turnover, lost clients, and a culture that stops caring. When buyers get this right, those same millions show up as retention, growth, and a team that leans into the future with you.

You don't need to be perfect. You just need to be present. Show up, tell the truth, and earn trust—one conversation at a time. To assist, with the QR code you have my Integration Checklist that has a section for HR related activities.

THE BEAUTIFUL CHAOS OF INTEGRATION

WHEN THE DEAL FINALLY CLOSES . . . AND REAL LIFE BEGINS

The wires hit. Signatures dried. Cheers all around. LinkedIn lit up with glossy posts about "the exciting next chapter."

The seller leaned back, a long breath escaping—decades of sweat and sacrifice finally cashed in. The buyer grinned across the table, flush with pride, convinced the future was his. And then came day two.

Payroll ran. Half the deposits bounced.

The new HR system flagged missing forms—a handful of employees weren't paid at all.

Benefits enrollment froze midstream.

Customers called in, only to hear familiar account managers whisper, "I'm not sure who I work for anymore."

The loyal head of operations—the seller's right hand, the glue of the company—already handed in a quiet resignation.

Vendor contracts piled on desks unsigned.

The city called to say the buyer wasn't even licensed to operate.

The seller sat in his new office, stunned. He had thought the buyer was a seasoned M&A expert. Instead, he was watching a rookie unravel. The acquisition had been planned. But the integration? Forgotten.

THE LESSON

From the closing table to the first 100 days, integration is where deals either uncover millions or the millions go missing. It isn't paperwork. It's leadership. It's systems, contracts, people, and culture colliding all at once. When done well, integration is a bridge into sustainable growth. Done poorly, it bleeds profit, erodes trust, and dismantles the legacy you thought you secured.

The fix isn't complicated: show up with clarity, assign an integration leader, and refuse to let chaos write your story for you.

START MUCH EARLIER THAN YOU THINK

Most people think integration begins after the close. That's a myth. In reality, great integration starts the moment you first sit across the table from the seller. Every conversation is data. How do they talk about their team? The employees who keep the culture alive without needing a title? The agreements that are sealed with handshakes instead of signatures? The systems they swear "work fine" but you know will collapse if not stabilized on day one?

Integration is living inside diligence long before anyone calls it that. Buyers who pay attention here are already building their playbook—they just need to write it down. As a buyer, I kept an ongoing log of every observation: what to vet in diligence, what to prepare for in integration, and what was left unsaid that might come back later. Once the deal closed, weekly integration meetings with all stakeholders is key to successful integration.

INTEGRATION IS ITS OWN DISCIPLINE— NOT A SIDE HUSTLE

Integration isn't something you tack on to your to-do list. It is a discipline in its own right. Whether you assign it to a buy-side project manager, a trusted fractional advisor (like me) or you own it yourself—someone must take responsibility. Bumbling through this phase will cost you immediate money, and worse, it will erode trust with your employees and customers, costing so much more down the road.

For sellers: this is where you matter most. You know where the skeletons are hidden—the vendor quirks, the payroll work-arounds, the files only your office manager knows how to find.

> GOOD INTEGRATION STARTS THE MOMENT YOU FIRST SIT ACROSS THE TABLE FROM THE SELLER.

Your wisdom is your employees' stability. Stepping in here doesn't weaken your negotiating position—it strengthens your legacy.

Some of the smoothest exits I've seen are not the ones with the highest multiples or the flashiest announcements. They're the ones where the seller stayed engaged just long enough to steady the ship and walk their people across the bridge with dignity.

THE FRONT LINES

In one acquisition I worked on, the seller stood in front of forty-five employees for the kickoff meeting. He didn't shrink from the moment—he leaned into it. He spoke with strength and sincerity, praised the buyer, and shared his hopes for the future. The room exhaled.

Because he had earned their trust over years of leadership, the team followed his lead, and the handoff began on solid ground.

But here's where it gets interesting. The seller had one request: he didn't want the team's day-to-day processes to change. He wanted to preserve what worked. Out of respect, we honored that—at first.

What happened? Within a year, the employees themselves began to push back. They wanted structure. They wanted new tools and opportunities. They wanted to operate like part of a larger organization. Change came anyway—just on their terms.

The lesson stayed with me: change delayed is not change avoided. It is simply deferred, and often harder later. In this case, we were lucky.

HOLLI'S RULE: THE "F" WORD

In M&A, the dirtiest "F" word isn't what you think—it's *fear*. Fear of change. Fear of friction. Fear of being the one who rocks the boat. Fear is far costlier than honesty. It paralyzes leadership and traps teams in limbo. Integration limbo is where morale rots, customers drift, and millions quietly leak out the back door.

So, my rule is simple: if you catch yourself dodging a decision because you're afraid of upsetting someone or "messing up the momentum," stop. Rethink. Then lead. Because in M&A, the only "F" word worse than *fear* . . . is *failure*.

THE NINE ESSENTIALS OF INTEGRATION PLANNING

Now, let me offer a strategic lens for a seamless transition. Integration is not about checking boxes—it's about ensuring the heart of the business still beats after the deal. However, over the years, I've built detailed integration checklists (yours through the QR code). But I kept seeing people get lost in the weeds—jumping from payroll systems to vendor files without ever stepping back to look at the whole picture.

So, I created the I.N.T.E.G.R.A.T.E. Framework to help both buyers and sellers stay grounded in the human, operational, and cultural story of integration.

Each letter represents a must-consider area and serves as a reminder that integration is as much art as it is execution. This is your strategic compass before the checklists start flying. It is the nine essentials I have seen work, whether the deal is $2 million or $200 million. Each letter is a reminder of what you cannot afford to miss.

HOLLI'S I.N.T.E.G.R.A.T.E. FRAMEWORK™

I—Identify the People
- Who are the leaders?
- Who quietly hold the trust of the staff?
- Build your employee retention plan long before closing.

N—Navigate the Culture
- What is their leadership style?
- Is this a culture match—or one that needs blending?
- Plan your messaging thoughtfully.

T—Tackle the Systems
- Payroll. Benefits. CRM. Operations
- IT systems, data migrations, security
- Identify system conflicts early—before they break post-close.

E—Empower the Seller to Help
- Sellers: You are the keeper of the institutional knowledge. Do not sit back—lean in.
- Buyers: Pull the seller in early and often. Their fingerprints are on every piece of this business. Use that wisdom while you can.
- Who decides what? New governance clarity.

G—Guard the Customers
- Proactively plan communication with your top clients.
- Who may feel unsettled by the change?
- Who needs early reassurance?

R—Review the Vendors
- Which contracts transfer?
- Are vendors locked in, or will they need negotiation?
- Capture the handshake deals that are not on paper.

A—Align Legal & Compliance
- Make sure licenses, filings, and permits are properly transitioned.
- These items can halt business if overlooked.

T—Track KPIs (Key Performance Indicators)
Track the health of the business:
- Revenue stability
- Customer retention

- Employee turnover
- Gross margin
- Cash forecast
- Pipeline conversion
Post-close KPIs tell you if the machine you bought is performing as expected.

E—Execute Communication Plans
- Employees. Vendors. Customers.
- Everyone needs a clear plan: who contacts them, what message is delivered and what is the timing of the communication.

Over-communicate. I used to think over-communicating was bad. It is not. Silence creates anxiety.

> DISCIPLINE IS NOT A PERSONALITY TRAIT—IT IS A DAILY CHOICE.

YOU DO NOT HAVE TO DO THIS ALONE

Too many buyers try to white-knuckle integration, thinking they will save money by doing it all themselves. But integration is where deals either flourish or fail, and failure is expensive. You do not need a ten-person private equity army, but you do need the right voices in the room: the CFO who sees around corners. The HR lead who spots people risks. The attorney who knows what is enforceable, not just what is written. The IT pro who can stop a payroll system crash before it happens. This is your team.

For Buyers:

- CFO or financial advisor
- HR specialist
- Legal counsel
- Systems/IT consultant
- Industry-specific operator

But what if you are a small business buyer without a big bench? You are not out of luck—you just need to be more intentional. Here's what you can do:

- Hire specialized M&A consultants and attorneys (even fractional)
- Use the INTEGRATE Framework to stay focused on what matters most
- Leverage the Integration Checklist to guide every step.

You do not need ten people—but you do need the right strategy, support, and intention.

For Sellers:

- Stay actively involved
- Help build the integration roadmap
- Protect your team while guiding your buyer

Even with small deals, private equity firms often have six to ten people on diligence and integration calls. You do not need their headcount—but you do need their discipline. Integration is where your deal gets real. Having the right support is how you make it work.

THE DISCIPLINE THAT BUILDS EMPIRES

Integration success is rarely about technical knowledge. It is about leadership, preparation, and discipline. Disciplined planning. Disciplined communication. Disciplined execution. That's where empires are built—or where millions quietly go missing.

Diligence gets you to the closing table and integration determines whether the deal was worth doing. I've seen plenty of transactions close successfully only to bleed value in the months that followed. Missed handoffs, silence with employees, sloppy system transitions—it is not the headline mistakes that usually cost you, but the accumulation of smaller ones. And those missed details don't just cost money; they cost trust, momentum, and opportunity. Start integration planning early and do not go it alone.

Sellers—your role does not end at signing. You hold the knowledge that makes your people feel steady and your legacy endure.

Buyers—your discipline compounds with every deal. Integration is how one transaction becomes a platform, and a platform becomes an empire.

A personal note: Earlier in my career, I saw first-hand what happens when integration is left to chance. The intentions were good. The ambitions were bold. But the lack of structure meant that results shifted with the wind—and millions of dollars slipped quietly off the table.

Then I met Adam Coffey. His books, his mentorship, his discipline sharpened my perspective. He showed me that integration is not luck—it's process, precision, and persistence. Discipline is not a personality trait—it is a daily choice. And when it comes to integration, that choice is the difference between buying a business... and building an empire.

THE BOTTOM LINE

Diligence gets you to closing. Integration decides whether the millions you thought you bought stay in your pocket or quietly leak out the back door. This is how empires are built, and legacies are protected.

Every deal carries risk, but the goal is always the same—maximize value and minimize regret. Use the QR code to receive the Integration Checklist and the I.N.T.E.G.R.A.T.E. Framework™ to help you put this chapter into practice.

CHAPTER 16

RUN, FORREST, RUN!

M&A RED FLAGS THAT SHOULD SEND YOU RUNNING OUT THE DOOR.

A flag is on the field.

It was her first acquisition. She was excited and a little nervous, but ready.

The LOI was signed. Advisors were lined up. She dreamed of her celebration party. Then diligence began.

At first, documents trickled in: insurance policies, vendor contracts, but none of the really important stuff. Weeks passed. Still no balance sheet. No monthly P&L. Just promises that "It's coming."

She called again. More delays. The seller was "busy." The broker was "compiling." And that's when her gut said what her mouth couldn't: something was wrong. But what was it? Is this a red flag or yellow flag or is she just being paranoid?

RED, YELLOW, AND GREEN FLAGS

In this section, we won't be talking about spreadsheets. These flags are about behavior. The big-picture story and the way the seller tells (or avoids telling) it.

My friend GG had a saying, "Holli, when the audio and the visual don't match, there's something going on." Bam! Thanks GG. That's M&A in a nutshell.

When the seller's story doesn't line up with the numbers, or the numbers never show up at all—you've spotted your first red flag. One missing issue may be nothing; two might be coincidence. Three is a pattern. And patterns are what matter. Yet, most buyers ignore patterns or they don't know how to decipher the story the pattern is telling. They rationalize. They minimize. They press on because they want the deal. I get it. Hope is louder than fear when you've fallen in love with a business or you're just worn out from looking!

But the disciplined buyer is the one who knows how to read those flags, rank them, and walk away when needed. That's the buyer who builds empires.

This chapter will help you become that kind of buyer—the bloodhound who can sniff out the red flags, call them out, and know when to run before the missing millions run away from you. And I cannot forget about my sellers because understanding red flags means you won't be waving any around, which impacts your value and your bottom line, too!

MY BACKGROUND: THE BLOODHOUND

A long time ago, in a land far, far away Holli was an auditor. Yes, I performed regular business audits and swiftly found myself in the midst of many fraud exams. Truth be told, I rather enjoyed it. Doing audits was like solving a mystery, and who doesn't love a great "who-dunnit" drama? I would raise my hand high to my boss to be assigned the task of solving the unsolvable with my trusty magnifying glass, spidey-sense, and a calculator that never lied. (Ok the magnifying glass was thrown in just for dramatic effect.)

In any case, beyond the numbers, there were always other clues. Like the sweet silver-haired bookkeeper on her second career after retiring as a schoolteacher. Everyone loved her and her homemade blueberry muffins, but nobody questioned why she pulled up to work in a new Mercedes S-Class. No golden pension. No hidden trust fund. Just fuzzy math and a creative definition of a "bonus."

"They'll never miss it," she told herself, smoothing the numbers, tucking her trail neatly into the books. And maybe she would've been right . . . until I came along and the heist was up!

Sadly, every time I have discovered fraud, the perpetrator was the most trusted advisor. This is why I always read the story in the financials— and just as importantly, I read the people. Think of me as the M&A version of the airport dog that sniffs out explosives. (But considerably more fashionable.) Because that's exactly what buried deal risk feels like: hidden explosives inside a glossy offer package.

> SADLY, EVERY TIME I HAVE DISCOVERED FRAUD, THE PERPETRATOR WAS THE MOST TRUSTED ADVISOR.

Believe me, I've seen all the common tricks in the books—literally. There is the vanishing equity trick: profits every year, yet somehow equity never grows. Where's it all going? Then, there is the 180 days of A/R. If it takes six months to collect, that's not receivables. That's a charity program—or something else.

Businesses come with plenty of normal risk. Customers leave, markets wobble, gold-star employees quit. That's enough. You don't need to stack *extra* risk on top because you didn't know how to read the flags–red, yellow or green.

Unless you're a professional turnaround artist—and let's be honest, 99% of buyers aren't—you don't want a fixer-upper. You want a solid business that runs cleanly.

Or at least, if you do walk into a mess, you want to know exactly where the mess is and how to mop it up before you step in it. That's not about being cautious. That's about being smart and exercising discipline.

BEHAVIORAL RED FLAGS

Behavior doesn't lie. When the story a seller tells doesn't match the way they act, that's when you lean in. You'll see it in the little things first: delays, stalling, over-explaining the small stuff while side-stepping the big questions. Sometimes it's tone—maybe defensiveness, the agitation, the way the energy shifts when diligence gets real.

Call it what it is, a red flag that must be chased down. It's the seller showing you something they may not want to put on paper. If they get prickly when you ask for basics, that *is* your disclosure.

Hey sellers: your story and your behavior *must* match. If you want the highest multiple, come prepared. Answer the big questions as directly as the small ones. Transparency isn't weakness—it's what builds confidence in your valuation. Buyers pay more for trust.

THE BROKER WHO DIDN'T WANT ME LOOKING

I was evaluating an accounting firm for acquisition. The broker controlled the LOI process. I had not yet even spoken to the seller. The broker provided a year-end P&L. But we were nine months into the new year. There were no monthly financials. No current P&L. No balance sheet. I told this earlier in the book but I left the dramatic ending for red flags chapter.

I asked for what any serious buyer would ask for: "Please send me a current balance sheet and year-to-date P&L." And that was the trigger. The broker shifted instantly. He got defensive. Animated. Agitated. "You're trying to start diligence right now . . . That's not how this works . . . You're jumping ahead of the process . . . I've done hundreds of deals, and you are asking for too much." I soon found out that he would not allow me to put forth an offer. There were too many buyers he said . . . And just like that, I was out.

WAS HE AN ANGEL OR DEVIL?

To me, that broker was an angel (some people might say he was another "A" word...). He saved me time and money. By the time that conversation ended, I already knew what was really happening. The seller had problems, the broker knew it, and I was too informed to be allowed near them. They needed a less educated buyer. I'm not that buyer and neither are you!

HOLLI'S TIP

If someone resists basic financial disclosure, that *is* your disclosure. Red Flag on the field. The kind of red flag that has you not just walking away but running away.

THE STORY OF BODY LANGUAGE GONE BAD

A few years back, I was doing QofE on a deal. The moment I started asking normal questions around related entities, the seller started squirming in his seat and actually raised his voice at me when I asked for more information.

None of those actions were normal and the broker made excuses, insinuating I was asking the wrong questions. The buyer took the bait because he was in fantasy land. I knew we were not dealing with someone with integrity. We pressed forward but not for long. Come to find out, I uncovered multiple entities and untraceable EBITDA. The seller was using related-party transactions to obscure the numbers. This is why you must always investigate related-party transactions fully. These are one of the most common hiding places for financial manipulation. In this case, the seller's behavior was not normal. This was a very big red flag.

> A MISSING BALANCE SHEET IS NOT JUST AN OVERSIGHT; IT'S A CLUE.

FINANCIAL RED FLAGS

Warren Buffett said it best: "Accounting is the language of business." If that's true, then red flags are bad grammar.

A missing balance sheet is not just an oversight; it's a clue. Annual summaries in place of monthly reports are not efficiency—it's camouflage. Addbacks that don't reconcile, tax returns that don't match the P&L, aging reports that drift from reality—each one is a breadcrumb leading you to either sloppiness or something far worse.

Here is Holli's rule that is worth tattooing on your deal journal: if the balance sheet is wrong, the P&L is wrong. Full stop.

I said it earlier, and I'll say it again. You're not nitpicking when you call this out. You're protecting yourself from buying numbers that don't exist.

And sellers, listen carefully: clean books sell for higher multiples. Period. Sloppy, late, or inconsistent financials do not just slow the deal—they devalue it. Buyers don't pay premiums for risk. They discount it. If you want top dollar, invest in a quality of earnings report before you go to market. It's your proof of integrity. If you can't reconcile your own numbers, the buyer will—and you won't like their version of the story.

STORY: THE TAX RETURN THAT SCREAMED

A firm's internal P&L didn't match the tax return by hundreds of thousands of dollars. When questioned, the seller admitted to deducting unrelated expenses— possibly from another company. This was not stretching the IRS boundaries. This very well could be considered fraud. Even in an asset deal, tax fraud exposure can leak through. And if the seller won't do it right on paper, what else are they hiding?

BUYER DANGER ZONES: EXCUSES

This is where I see buyers get into trouble—not because the red flags weren't there, but because they talked themselves into ignoring them. The soundtrack usually goes like this:

- "They're not great with numbers."
- "They've been busy—they'll get it to me."
- "It's just one small thing."
- "Everyone fudges a bit on taxes."

Nope. Stop right there. Every red flag is either isolated or systemic. And you won't know which until you actually dig in. If you shrug it off, you're not being flexible— you're being reckless.

CHAPTER 16

THE SMART SELLER'S PREP

Here's how savvy sellers get ahead:

- Have current, clean financials ready—monthly P&Ls, balance sheet, aging reports.
- Make sure your tax returns reconcile to your books.
- Be transparent about related party transactions—don't let the buyer discover them first.
- Have answers ready for basic cash flow and payroll questions.
- Keep your tone even. Curiosity from a buyer isn't an attack—it's diligence.

Your story and your numbers need to line up. When they do, you build confidence. Confidence gets you the highest possible multiple.

LEGAL AND STRUCTURAL RED FLAGS

People say, "it's just paperwork," until the paperwork blows up the deal. The bones of a business are in its legal structure. If those bones are weak, no amount of fancy dressing holds it up.

Watch for ownership that's unclear and outdated contracts. Intellectual property still in a founder's personal name. No employee IP/confidentiality agreements. Lawsuits or settlements never disclosed. Contractors treated like employees. No bylaws or operating agreement at all. If a seller resists providing governing documents or litigation/ IP schedules, that resistance *is* disclosure. Your attorney can help mitigate, but only if the issues are surfaced.

Hey sellers: Don't wait for diligence to uncover skeletons.

Clean up ownership records, employee agreements, and IP assignments *before* you list your business. Every missing document gives buyers a reason to question everything else. Tight structure signals discipline—and discipline earns multiples.

TEAM & CULTURE RED FLAGS

Spreadsheets don't run companies—people do. Culture tells you more than the numbers ever will. Red flags show up fast: key employees leaving mid-process, silence in the halls during site visits, senior staff "in the dark" about the sale, no second layer of management.

If you have access, ask employees how they are doing and if they can see their future in the new company. What worries them most about the company's future? Their words—and maybe more importantly, their body language which will tell you everything.

If the culture feels off, you're not imagining it. That unease you feel on the site visit is a signal. Don't ignore it. Numbers won't fix broken culture.

For Sellers: Your team is part of your valuation. If employees are blindsided or key leaders start are uneasy, it kills momentum and trust. Communicate thoughtfully, protect your people, and make sure they're part of the story. A stable, informed team is one of the strongest selling points you have.

WHEN SHOULD I WALK?

Some red flags can be mitigated; many yellow flags can accumulate to a red flag and some red flags become suspected fraud. How do you know when to walk? Not all red flags mean stop—but they always mean slow down, investigate, and decide. Use this framework to evaluate whether you're spotting fixable issues . . . or dodging bullets.

FRAMEWORK: THE RED FLAG TIERING SYSTEM

Tier	Type of Red Flag	Meaning	What to Do
Tier 1: **Cosmetic** **(yellow)**	Sloppy docs, poor formatting, minor mistakes	Normal disorganization, not usually deception	Fixable; proceed with caution, flag for cleanup. These items are typically normalized in a QofE report via EBITDA adjustments.
Tier 2: **Operational** **(Orange)**	Inconsistent numbers, delayed responses, aging or detailed reports missing or not matching the BS	Systemic weakness or overwhelm; sellers expect lower multiples	Add time & budget to diligence, request clarity. QofE is highly recommended—expect more adjustments and caveats. Plan for cleanup post-close if the deal proceeds. Tier 2 and tier 3 without mitigation could be potential fraud. Be willing to walk.

Tier	Type of Red Flag	Meaning	What to Do
Tier 3: Behavioral (Red)	Evasion, defensiveness, over explaining, contradictions between talk and numbers	Seller overwhelm, potential integrity issue, emotional resistance or hidden risk	Pause. Re-engage with empathy but rigor. Reassess. Let the QofE test your instincts: does it validate the story or unearth worse? Be willing to run.
Tier 4: Structural or Ethical (Black)	Tax fraud, co-mingled entities, refusal to share financials, suspected fraud	High likelihood of systemic risk you cannot fix.	Run, Forest, Run! You cannot model your way out of ethical failure. Or hiding through related entities. No indemnity clause is strong enough.

SELLERS: RED FLAGS GO BOTH WAYS

Red flags are not just for buyers. If you are selling your company—and especially if you are staying on post-close or tied to an earnout—you need to watch the buyer just as closely.

Words and actions must match.

If the buyer starts behaving differently in final negotiations—if promises get revised, if terms suddenly shift, if integrity feels like it's leaking from the conversation—these are your flags.

BEWARE OF SLIPPERY BUYERS

One of my clients was set to sell their business for eight figures to a private equity group. It was the kind of

187

deal that would change his life—forever. We were 30 days from close. The purchase agreement was in final markup. And then the buyer tried to materially change the earnout. No heads-up. No explanation. Just a sneaky shift of the goalposts. My client paused and looked at me and said, "If they'll do this now, what else will they do once they own us?" He being a courageous leader walked away from eight figures.

Because trust isn't a bonus term—it is the deal. And without it, you owe them nothing. But—we have a happy ending alert! The private equity firm had the weekend to think about it. Monday, they came back apologetic, aligned, and ready to restore trust. The earnout was returned to its original terms. The deal closed a few weeks later. And everyone walked away with what mattered most—dignity, clarity, and a future they could trust.

Sellers—Drawing a hard line does not always end the deal. Sometimes, it's exactly what earns you the right deal. And remember if the buyer shows you who they are, believe them.

THE BOTTOM LINE

The hardest part of any deal is admitting that a red flag is exactly what it looks like. Not a yellow. Not a maybe. A red. The disciplined buyers and sellers walk when trust breaks. The smart sellers prepare so they don't throw flags on themselves. Remember: you're not just buying or selling numbers—you're trading trust. See the flags. Respect them. And if you need to run, run early. That's not fear. That's discipline—and discipline builds empires.

CHAPTER 17

THE FINAL CHAPTER: GAME TIME

THE TALKING IS OVER, GET OUT THERE AND WIN!

The locker room smelled of sweat, leather, and anticipation. Helmets rested on benches, shoulder pads clattered as players shifted nervously, waiting for the signal. The scoreboard outside was dark for now, but everyone knew it wouldn't stay that way for long.

The coach stepped forward—calm, steady, eyes sharp. She didn't pace. She didn't shout. She simply looked at the team and began.

"You've trained for this. You've run the drills—you've ridden through canyons, mastered diligence, waltzed through working capital, played the value chessboard, and covered your tail insurance. You've studied the playbook—the P&L, the balance sheet, the cash flow statement. You've sparred with ghosts and liars, lovers and cowboys. Every rep in this book was practice. Every Mock-Tale conditioning. And now—it's game time."

A murmur rippled through the players. The coach's voice rose.

"Out there, it won't be clean. Deals never are. Numbers will lie if you let them. Emotions will try to rattle you. Opponents will come at you with pressure, distraction, and promises that don't hold. But stay focused. You're ready. You can read the field. You were born for this!"

She slammed her open hand against the whiteboard, rattling the room.

"This is your moment! Remember why you are here. Remember the goals you are after, the passion that ignites you, and the people who are counting on you.

Discipline is your muscle. Integrity your helmet. Strategy is your playbook. And numbers tell you everything you need to know. Don't freeze. Don't fumble. You know the play: minimize regret and maximize the value. Play the game with steady hands and a clear head."

The players leaned forward now, eyes locked, the tension breaking into fire as helmets snapped into place.

"This is your game. Your deal. Your tale. Your future. Go out there and find the missing millions. And write a story worth telling—your own!"

The whistle blew. The doors opened. The coach gave one final admonishment, "Now go out there and WIN!"

The team roared and rushed the doors. In a flash the locker room was still.

And the field—the future—was theirs.

Remember: *Numbers tell stories. Holli tells stories. Now you can too.*

The End

HOLLI'S M&A
SURVIVAL GLOSSARY

APA / SPA: Asset Purchase Agreement / Stock Purchase Agreement. The final legal contract to sell either assets (APA) or company stock (SPA or EPA).
Holli's Version: The actual marriage license—the paperwork that makes the deal official.

Arbitrage: Buying smaller companies at lower valuation multiples and selling the combined entity at a higher multiple.
Holli's Version: Buying at 3x and selling at 8x—the spread is the profit magic.

Asset Deal: A transaction where the buyer purchases specific assets (and sometimes liabilities) rather than the entire legal entity. This transaction culminates in an APA.
Holli's Version: Buying the house, not the whole neighborhood.

Buy Box: A defined set of criteria a buyer uses to identify ideal acquisition targets (size, industry, geography, etc.).
Holli's Version: Your shopping list for deals—what you want and what you'll walk away from.

CapEx (Capital Expenditures): Funds used to acquire, maintain, or improve long-term assets such as property or equipment.
Holli's Version: The company's big-ticket purchases—like a facelift for the business.

Carve-Out: When a parent company sells a division, product line, or subsidiary, separating it from the larger organization.
Holli's Version: Cutting a slice of the business to sell on its own.

CIM (Confidential Information Memorandum): A detailed presentation prepared by the seller or seller's broker that provides financial, operational, and market information to potential buyers.
Holli's Version: The company's dating profile—all the highlights, none of the mess.

Claw Back: A contractual right allowing money already paid to be recovered under certain conditions.
Holli's Version: A refund clause—if things go south, money comes back.

Closing: The final step in the transaction when ownership officially transfers.
Holli's Version: Deal Day—money moves, papers are signed, and champagne (sometimes) pops.

Core Earnings: Recurring, sustainable profits from normal operations, excluding one-time or unusual items.
Holli's Version: The steady-state profit—the version of EBITDA that reflects the business as it truly runs.

Data Room: A secure online repository for sharing due-diligence documents during a transaction.
Holli's Version: The digital vault for all documents until the deal closes.

Deal Structure: How the transaction is organized—cash, seller notes, earnouts, equity rollovers, etc.
Holli's Version: The architecture of the deal—how the money and risk are built.

Diligence: The buyer's deep review of financial, legal, HR and operational information before closing.
Holli's Version: The background check before you say "I do."

E&O Coverage (Errors and Omissions Insurance): Insurance that protects professionals from claims of negligence or inadequate work.
Holli's Version: Your safety net when a detail gets missed.

EBIT: Earnings Before Interest and Taxes—a measure of operating profit.
Holli's Version: Profit before borrowing costs and the taxman show up.

EBITDA: Earnings Before Interest, Taxes, Depreciation, and Amortization—a key measure of profit often used to value a business.
Holli's Version: Profit before you factor in debt, taxes, or accounting stuff like depreciation.

Earnout: A contingent payment based on the business hitting performance targets after closing.
Holli's Version: A bonus that only gets paid if the business hits its goals after sale.

Enterprise Value (EV): The total value of a business's operations, including both debt and equity, minus excess cash. It reflects what a buyer would pay for the entire

company as a whole—before deciding how the purchase is financed. Often used interchangeably with MVIC (Market Value of Invested Capital).
Holli's Version: The headline number—what the business is worth in total before paying off debt or handing cash back to the owner.

EPA (Estimated Purchase Agreement): A legal contract documenting the sale and transfer of ownership of a company's equity (shares). Functionally the same as a Stock Purchase Agreement (SPA).
Holli's Version: The contract that transfers ownership of the company's shares—same as an SPA.

Force Multiplier: Something that amplifies results beyond the effort applied.
Holli's Version: The secret ingredient that turns good growth into explosive growth.

GAAP (Generally Accepted Accounting Principles): Standardized accounting rules used in the United States to ensure consistency in financial reporting.
Holli's Version: The rulebook accountants live by.

Holdbacks (Indemnity / Escrow): Indemnity is the seller's obligation to cover post-closing claims or losses. Escrow is money held by a third party to secure that promise. A holdback is the portion of the purchase price the buyer keeps directly for the same reason for a period of time.
Holli's Version: The deal's safety net—promises backed by money set aside until the dust settles.

Integration: The process of combining operations, systems, and teams after a deal closes.
Holli's Version: This is where strategy becomes reality. Integration determines whether the projected value actually shows up—it's less about kumbaya and more about aligning people, processes, and priorities so the business functions as one.

LOI / IOI: Letter of Intent / Indication of Interest. Outlines proposed terms before a purchase agreement; usually non-binding except for a few clauses.
Holli's Version: The engagement before the marriage—serious, but you can still walk away.

Market EBITDA Multiple: The typical valuation multiple paid for companies of similar size and industry in the market.
Holli's Version: What buyers are paying this season.

Multiple of Earnings: The multiplier applied to EBITDA or SDE to calculate business value.
Holli's Version: The "how many times profit" number that sets the price tag.

MVIC (Market Value of Invested Capital): The total value of a business—equal to enterprise value. It represents what the entire company is worth before factoring in how it's financed or who gets paid (lenders or owners).
Holli's Version: The business's full market value—the number you get before subtracting debt or adding cash.

Normalized or Adjusted EBITDA: EBITDA adjusted to remove non-recurring, discretionary, or non-operational items to reflect sustainable earnings.
Holli's Version: The cleaned-up profit number.

Operating Earnings: Profit from a company's core business activities—before interest and taxes are applied. Often used interchangeably with EBIT.
Holli's Version: The company's true operating profit—what the business earns from running itself, before the bank or the IRS take their share.

Ordinary Income: Income subject to standard tax rates, as opposed to capital gains rates.
Holli's Version: Regular income—nothing fancy, just fully taxable.

PE (Private Equity): Investment firms that buy and grow companies using a mix of equity and debt, often aiming to sell later at a higher valuation.
Holli's Version: The pros who buy, fix, and flip businesses—with other people's money.

QoE (Quality of Earnings): A report analyzing if profits are accurate, consistent, and sustainable.
Holli's Version: A financial truth check.

Reps & Warranties: Legal promises in the purchase agreement about the accuracy of information provided.
Holli's Version: The seller's long list of promises—all written down by lawyers in the purchase agreement.

Reps and Warranties Insurance: Insurance that covers losses from breaches of reps and warranties in the purchase agreement.
Holli's Version: The safety net when promises get broken.

Retrade: When a buyer attempts to renegotiate a reduction in the purchase price after due diligence uncovers issues.
Holli's Version: The post-inspection discount.

SDE (Seller's Discretionary Earnings): Profit plus the owner's salary and perks.
Holli's Version: What the business makes if you step into the owner's shoes.

Seller Note: A loan from the seller to the buyer for part of the purchase price.
Holli's Version: When the seller plays banker to help you buy their company.

SMB (Small and Medium-Sized Business): Privately held companies typically with less than $100 million in revenue.
Holli's Version: The heartbeat of the economy—where most deals happen.

Stock Deal: A transaction where the buyer purchases shares of the company's stock and assumes all assets and liabilities.
Holli's Version: Buying the whole neighborhood not just a house.

Synergies: Cost savings or revenue growth expected when two companies combine.
Holli's Version: The magic math buyers put in pitch decks—sometimes real, sometimes wishful thinking.

Tail Insurance: Extended insurance coverage for claims that arise after a policy ends.
Holli's Version: The ghostbuster of deals—protects you from skeletons that come out after closing.

Tax Shield (CapEx): Tax savings that result from deducting depreciation or other expenses related to capital assets.
Holli's Version: The silver lining—spend on assets, pay less in taxes.

Top-Line Sales: Total revenue generated before deducting expenses.
Holli's Version: Ditto.

Trailing Twelve Months (TTM): The past twelve months of financial performance, used to measure recent results.
Holli's Version: The freshest snapshot—the last 12 months tell the real story.

True-Up: A post-closing adjustment to align estimates with actual results (e.g., working capital or earnout).
Holli's Version: The final scorecard—where you check if everyone paid or got paid fairly.

Turnarounds: Situations where an underperforming business is restructured and revitalized to improve profitability.
Holli's Version: 10% or less net income as a percentage of revenue.

Valuation: The process of determining what a business is worth, often using multiples or discounted cash flow.
Holli's Version: The price tag—what someone is willing to pay and someone is willing to accept.

Working Capital: Current assets (cash, receivables, inventory) minus current liabilities (payables, accruals).
Holli's Version: The oxygen of the business—keeps day-to-day operations alive.

Working Capital Peg: The agreed "normal" level of work-ing capital the business needs at closing.
Holli's Version: The agreed fuel level—enough gas in the tank when the business changes hands.

A Personal Request from the Author

Dear Reader,

If this book moved you, taught you something new,
or simply kept you turning the pages,
would you take a moment to leave a review on Amazon?

Your feedback helps other readers discover the book—
and it means the world to me as an author.

Thank you for being part of this journey.

SILVERSMITH
PRESS

Serves new and emerging authors
to help them write, publish, and promote their books.
Are you ready to share your story?

Visit us!
www.silversmithpress.com

www.ingramcontent.com/pod-product-compliance
Lightning Source LLC
Chambersburg PA
CBHW042120190326
41519CB00031B/7557